The Best War Ever

Also by Sheldon Rampton and John Stauber

Banana Republicans

Weapons of Mass Deception

Trust Us, We're Experts!

Mad Cow U.S.A.

Toxic Sludge Is Good for You!

The Best War Ever

Lies, Damned Lies, and
the Mess in Iraq

SHELDON RAMPTON
and **JOHN STAUBER**

JEREMY P. TARCHER / PENGUIN
A MEMBER OF PENGUIN GROUP (USA) INC.
NEW YORK

JEREMY P. TARCHER/PENGUIN
Published by the Penguin Group
Penguin Group (USA) Inc., 375 Hudson Street, New York, New York 10014,
USA • Penguin Group (Canada), 90 Eglinton Avenue East, Suite 700,
Toronto, Ontario M4P 2Y3, Canada (a division of Pearson Penguin Canada Inc.)
• Penguin Books Ltd, 80 Strand, London WC2R 0RL, England • Penguin
Ireland, 25 St Stephen's Green, Dublin 2, Ireland (a division of Penguin
Books Ltd) • Penguin Group (Australia), 250 Camberwell Road, Camberwell,
Victoria 3124, Australia (a division of Pearson Australia Group Pty Ltd) •
Penguin Books India Pvt Ltd, 11 Community Centre, Panchsheel Park,
New Delhi–110 017, India • Penguin Group (NZ), Cnr Airborne and Rosedale
Roads, Albany, Auckland 1310, New Zealand (a division of Pearson New
Zealand Ltd) • Penguin Books (South Africa) (Pty) Ltd, 24 Sturdee Avenue,
Rosebank, Johannesburg 2196, South Africa

Penguin Books Ltd, Registered Offices:
80 Strand, London WC2R 0RL, England

Most Tarcher/Penguin books are available at special quantity discounts for bulk
purchase for sales promotions, premiums, fund-raising, and educational needs.
Special books or book excerpts also can be created to fit specific needs. For details, write Penguin Group (USA) Inc. Special Markets, 375 Hudson Street,
New York, NY 10014.

ISBN 1-58542-509-5

Printed in the United States of America
1   3   5   7   9   10   8   6   4   2

BOOK DESIGN BY LOVEDOG STUDIO

Contents

Acknowledgments

We thank our employer, the nonprofit educational organization Center for Media and Democracy, and the individuals and nonprofit foundations who have supported its work since 1993. This book is part of the Center's unique mission of investigating propaganda as it is waged by corporations and governments. For information on the Center, visit its website at www.prwatch.org, or contact its office: 520 University Avenue, Suite 227, Madison, Wisconsin 53703; phone (608) 260-9713.

Many thanks to Laura Miller, former editor of the Center's quarterly *PR Watch*. Some of Laura's research and writing is included in our opening chapter, "The Victory of Spin." Thanks also to Diane Farsetta, the Center's senior researcher, and to Bob Burton, who edits our SourceWatch website (www.source watch.org), for their ideas and research contributions, as well as to Center staffers Patricia Barden, Jonathan Rosenblum, Judith Siers-Poisson, and Sari Williams, without whose contributions we would not have had the time to produce this book.

Thanks especially to our editor, Mitch Horowitz, whose invaluable advice, encouragement, and good sense have helped more than we can say. Thanks also to Tarcher/Penguin publisher Joel Fotinos and publicity director Ken Siman.

The following individuals have helped us with ideas, comments, research, and other support: Chris Albritton, Aaron Glantz, Peter Sluglett, Jim Kavanagh, and Walda Wood.

John thanks his colleague Sheldon for tackling most of the research and writing of this book.

The Best War Ever

The Innocents Abroad

IN NOVEMBER 2003—ABOUT THE TIME THAT THE initial euphoria of war began to fade in the United States—*Newsweek* magazine reported a startling fact about the tactics Iraqi guerrillas used against U.S. soldiers: "In Iraq, when guerrillas place an IED (improvised explosive device) by the side of the road, they sometimes write a warning on the street—in Arabic. The locals understand to steer clear; the Americans drive right into the trap. 'Everyone knows about it except us,' grouses Lieutenant Julio Tirado of the 124th Infantry Regiment, Florida National Guard, patrolling warily in the town of Ramadi."[1]

The story reminded us of an unrelated incident that we happened to witness back in the United States, when we took a trip that required flying on a small commuter airplane. The plane had only a single bathroom, and it had a note taped to the door that said "Out of order."

On the same plane, we noticed another traveler—a woman, dressed in a non-Western white robe that suggested she was from some country in Asia or the Middle East. She was traveling alone and apparently did not know how to speak any English. After the flight got under way, she got up to use the bathroom. She tried the door, but it wouldn't open. The note on the door was written in English, so she couldn't read it. She tried the door again. She looked around at the other passengers and said something in her native language, which no one understood. People tried to tell her that the bathroom was broken, but she didn't understand a word they said. People tried hand gestures, also to no avail. The concept of "broken" is simple and easily understood in any language, but there is no universal hand gesture for it. No one was able to communicate. Eventually she simply gave up in frustration and returned to her seat.

The incident made us think about our own experiences traveling in foreign countries—not in countries like England or Mexico, where English is either the native language or is widely spoken in tourist areas—but in countries like Turkey and Japan, where our own ability to communicate was every bit as limited as that of the woman on the plane. Simple tasks such as ordering food in a restaurant, buying batteries, or asking for directions became nearly impossible.

Imagine for a moment that the woman on the airplane were suddenly placed in charge of running a major city in the United States. Would she be able to handle the job? That is essentially the situation in which U.S. troops find themselves in Iraq. They don't simply lack an understanding of Iraq's history and culture, they lack even the language skills needed to communicate about basic, simple things. The enemies they are fighting do not need to be particularly intelligent to outmaneuver them, and they certainly don't need to be noble. (Indeed, they are not.) The mere fact that they can speak the native language confers a huge advantage over U.S. forces, which cannot be overcome by mere money and technology, let alone by the arrogance that has been America's main defense against the realization that the war in Iraq was a mistake.

On November 15, 2005, *Wall Street Journal* reporter Greg Jaffe told the story of David (last name withheld for security reasons), a U.S. Army foreign-affairs officer stationed undercover in northwestern Iraq. David wore civilian clothes and was so fluent in Arabic that the locals thought he was one of them. As a result, he was able to tell American military commanders how jihadist fighters had moved into Iraq across the Syrian border. He advised commanders and other officials on how to deal with their Iraqi counterparts and fired incompetent interpreters who had been hired by officials who didn't know the language. But here's the catch: he was one of only a handful of U.S. soldiers with those skills, and the military was in the process of pulling him out of Iraq. According to Colonel John D'Agostino, who oversaw his unit, "When David leaves, the U.S. Embassy's regional office in Mosul won't have a single Arabic speaker or Middle Eastern expert on its staff."[2]

This shocking deficit is a reflection of one of the central yet rarely mentioned paradoxes about the role that the United States has come to occupy in the world. No other nation on earth is as involved in the affairs of other countries, yet the American people show very little knowledge of or even interest in knowing about those countries and their cultures. Hundreds of thousands of American troops are stationed on more than eight hundred military installations scattered throughout the world, and currently the United States is simultaneously fighting two wars, in Iraq and Afghanistan. Yet whereas many citizens of Europe learn to speak several languages by the time they are adults, most people in the United States are lucky if they pick up even a smattering of French or German by the time they graduate from school. When large numbers of Hispanic immigrants began arriving in Florida and the U.S. southwest a couple of decades ago, the backlash included efforts to pass English-only laws that would restrict the immigrants' abilities to do business and communicate publicly in their native language.

Under the Bush administration, this combination of cultural isolationism and imperial ambition has taken political form as unilateralism—the odd notion that the United States can invade and successfully occupy a country as far away and as alien to American understanding as Iraq, without listening to or obtaining agreement and support from its own major allies, let alone from the people and nations of the Middle East. A few months before the war began, then House majority leader Tom DeLay was interviewed by Fox News correspondent John Gibson. "You know," Gibson said, "experts such as Henry Kissinger, Lawrence Eagleburger, have said . . . you should get many countries as allies on board first. Should we?"

"We're no longer a superpower. We're a super-duper-power," DeLay replied. He added, "We are the leader that defends freedom and democracy around the world. We are the leader in the war on terrorism. When we lead, others will follow."[3]

Nearly four years have passed since those words were uttered, and reality is beginning to sink in. The carefully constructed images of invincibility, victory, and triumph that attended the onset of war have lost much of their power to persuade. Our previous book *Weapons of Mass Deception* began and ended with two of those iconic moments that, at the time, seemed to many people to capture the stunning success of Bush's war in Iraq: the toppling of Saddam Hussein's statue in Firdos Square, and Bush's "mission accomplished" speech aboard a U.S. aircraft carrier, in which he declared an end to "major combat" in Iraq. We wrote that "the situation is more complicated than the images of victory that looked so unambiguously inspiring on American television. It is important, therefore, that we ask ourselves what lies behind those images, how they were constructed, and what they may be hiding."[4]

Today, we know much more about how those images were constructed. According to a U.S. Army assessment report, for example, the toppling of Saddam Hussein's statue was actually orchestrated by an army psychological operations ("psy-ops") unit.[5] And rather than the "end to major combat" that Bush promised, we have seen continuing and escalating violence. When Bush was filmed flying onto that aircraft carrier, commentators predicted that his reelection team would want to use the footage in future campaign commercials. By 2004, however, the "mission accomplished" speech had become an embarrassment for the administration, and by 2005 a majority of Americans were telling pollsters that the war was a mistake.

A number of reasons can be offered for the unraveling of U.S. support for the war: the admission by the White House that its claims about Iraqi weapons of mass destruction and links to Al Qaeda were false, the embarrassment of Abu Ghraib, the mounting human and economic cost of war. Together, they demonstrate that reality always bats last in politics, as it does in the rest of life. Propaganda may sometimes lead people and nations astray, but, as Abraham Lincoln observed, "You can fool some of the people all of the time, and all of the people some of the time, but you can't fool all of the people all of the time."

One of the saddest realities about Iraq is that the American people have had to relearn a lesson they already learned during the Vietnam War: that the nation's leaders, like the leaders of other countries, are capable of misleading the public even with respect to matters of life-and-death importance. The mess in Iraq also ought to teach us a lasting lesson about the dangers of believing our own propaganda. America entered Iraq with the belief that its moral, technological, and military superiority—its "super-duperhood"—would ensure victory. Instead, it found a morass of problems that do not lend themselves to ethical, technological, or military solutions—especially in a country whose language and culture are so different from its own. Paul Bremer, the U.S.-appointed head of the coalition occupation authority during the first year of the occupation, had never set foot in Iraq until the day he arrived to start running the country, and he did not even know how to speak Arabic. During his time in Iraq, he took daily lessons in the language, and shortly before his return to the United States, he expressed satisfaction that he was finally starting to understand the gist of conversations.[6] Is it surprising that Bremer would admit, a year and a half later, that "we really didn't see the insurgency coming"?[7] America's cultural isolationism carries a heavy price. If Americans cannot understand the rest of the world, they cannot hope to successfully engage with it, let alone to lead.

We are writing this book in the hope that this lesson, learned once again at great cost, will this time be fully appreciated and never again forgotten.

CHAPTER ONE

The Victory of Spin

ON THE SUNDAY BEFORE THANKSGIVING 2005, President George W. Bush delivered a speech to cadets at the United States Naval Academy. The podium stood flanked by posters that featured the phrase "Plan for Victory" in faux-embossed gold letters against a blue backdrop and the official seal of the academy. Behind him, the words "Plan for Victory" were repeated again on a large banner. The word "victory" was repeated fifteen times in the speech itself, and also figured prominently in an accompanying National Security Council document released by the White House to the press, titled *National Strategy for Victory in Iraq*.[1]

Bush's speech to cadets was the first in a series of five speeches aimed at countering charges that the war was going badly, delivered at a time when his popularity in opinion polls had fallen for the first time to about 40 percent.[2] Each speech was presented to a carefully chosen sympathetic audience, and the president took no questions afterward. The speeches culminated in a prime-time televised address from the Oval Office on Sunday, December 18—a week before Christmas, and timed to occur just days after the most successful elections in Iraq's history, in which an estimated ten million voters participated. It was the president's first prime-time address to the nation since he announced the commencement of war in Iraq thirty-three months earlier. But notwithstanding the Christmas season and the seemingly auspicious moment in Iraq, it was much more subdued than the speech Bush gave at the beginning of the war. Bush spent part of his time acknowledging mistakes and problems, and part of his time arguing with the mounting chorus of critics who, he said, "conclude that the war is lost." At times, the speech took on a pleading tone: "The need for victory is larger than any president or political party because the security of our people is in the balance," he said. "I do not expect you to support everything I do, but tonight I have a request: Do not give in to despair and do not give up on this fight for freedom."[3]

"Victory," of course, is something that every nation proclaims as the objective when it goes to war (although, inevitably, war ends in defeat or mutual ruination for most nations that engage in it). Bush's talk of victory in 2005, however, actually marked a *retreat* of sorts for a president who had declared "mission accomplished" two and a half years earlier. In a speech aboard the USS *Abraham Lincoln* in May 2003, Bush had told an audience of cheering troops that the United States could celebrate an "end" to "major combat operations in Iraq."[4] By contrast, his victory speeches at the end of 2005 were intended to shore up public opinion in the face of the indisputable fact that an end to combat was nowhere in sight.

The theme of "victory" was chosen, in fact, at the advice of Peter D. Feaver, a Duke University political scientist who had joined the National Security Council as a special adviser. Feaver's research at Duke focused on a problem he called "casualty aversion" or "casualty phobia"—his terms for the negative attitudes that Americans develop upon seeing their soldiers killed in war. He had analyzed opinion polls showing that public support for the war was slipping. Conventional wisdom suggested that the growing death toll and economic costs of the war were the reasons for the change in public opinion, but Feaver believed that this was only part of the story. According to the *New York Times*, he was recruited by the White House "after he and Duke colleagues presented to administration officials their analysis of polls about the Iraq war in 2003 and 2004. They concluded that Americans would support a war with mounting casualties on one condition: that they believe it would ultimately succeed."[5]

Bush's relentless repetition of the word "victory" was therefore part of a rhetorical strategy designed to extract further sacrifices from an increasingly jaundiced country. But aside from the word itself, Bush offered no definition of what "victory" meant, let alone a timetable for achieving it. To the contrary, the administration expressly rejected the idea of such a timetable. "We will not put a date certain on when each stage of success will be reached," stated the *National Strategy for Victory in Iraq*, "because the timing of success depends upon meeting certain conditions, not arbitrary timetables." The document was scattered with phrases such as "failure is not an option" and "our strategy for victory is clear," but the only time frames proposed for achieving U.S. objectives were virtually meaningless phrases: "short term," "medium term," and "longer term."[6]

There was no evidence that Bush's speeches had a significant effect on public opinion. A CNN/*USA Today*/Gallup poll found that only 10 percent of Americans watched or listened to it live, and only another 24 percent bothered to read or watch news reports about it after the fact. Afterward, only 41 percent believed that Bush had a plan for victory—virtually the same percentage that held that belief beforehand.[7] What little uptick he saw in opinion polls arguably reflected Americans' charitable mood during the holidays more than it reflected anything he actually said. By March 2006, his approval ratings had sunk to their lowest point since he took office. Gallup reported that only 32 percent of Americans believed Bush had a clear plan for Iraq, while 67 percent believed he did not.[8]

Best-Laid Plans

For some former supporters of the war, the irony was that the Bush administration had a plan available to implement for managing post-Saddam Iraq, but threw it out. During the year leading up to the war, the U.S. State Department had organized a Future of Iraq Project, which brought together seventeen teams, including 240 Iraqis, that produced two thousand pages of detailed reports including plans for health, education, sanitation, the economy, and postwar security. Some of their advice looked prophetic in retrospect, such as their prediction of widespread looting and insurgency once Saddam Hussein's regime fell. Shortly before the war began, however, these recommendations were shelved, and an entirely new team was brought in, which made a point of excluding people who had worked on the Future of Iraq Project as well as Pentagon officials with actual experience in postwar reconstructions. The fear, according to a Defense Department official, was that such people would offer pessimistic scenarios, which might leak to the press and undermine public support for the war.[9]

David Phillips, a former senior policy adviser to the Bush administration who worked on the Future of Iraq Project, resigned from the U.S. Department of State on September 11, 2003, to protest what he called "the terrible fiasco in Iraq." According to Phillips,

What was most astonishing about our postwar plan for Iraq isn't the plan with which we went to war; it is that we went to war with no plan at all. . . . For ideological reasons, the Office of the Secretary of Defense and the Office of the Vice President ignored, and even took steps to undermine, the Future of Iraq Project. . . . Instead of following the advice of these Iraqis and of experts who were involved in that planning process, the Bush administration chose instead to follow the advice of a small group of Iraqi exiles, led by Ahmed Chalabi, and to believe their own propaganda, which was that you could transform Iraq into a liberal democracy overnight, and that would then become the engine for reform in the Middle East. . . . The original belief was that we would be in and out of Iraq in ninety days.[10]

Paradoxically, the current mess in Iraq is a consequence of the brilliant marketing campaign originally waged by the Bush administration to sell the war to the American people—a campaign so successful that the war planners came to "believe their own propaganda." It gives us no pleasure to point out that we predicted this could happen, but we did. In March 2003, shortly before the war began, we posted an online essay that contained the following warning:

> Propaganda is often more successful at indoctrinating the propagandists themselves than it is at influencing the thinking of others. The discipline of "ensuring message consistency" cannot hope to succeed at controlling the world's perceptions of something as broad, sprawling and contradictory as the Bush administration's foreign policy. However, it may be successful at enabling people like George W. Bush and Donald Rumsfeld to ignore the warnings coming from Europe and other quarters. As our leaders lose their ability to listen to critics, we face the danger that they will underestimate the risks and costs involved in going to war. . . .
>
> No one with any knowledge of history or politics would expect today's leaders to behave in a perfectly moral fashion.

Few politicians have ever done that, and perhaps they never will. However, we should expect them at the very least to know what they are doing, and as the Bush administration traps itself within the mirrored echo chamber of its own propaganda, the danger increases that it will miscalculate, with catastrophic consequences for the United States and the world.[11]

The Power of Propaganda

"Propaganda," the British author Francis M. Cornford once quipped, "is that branch of the art of lying which consists in very nearly deceiving your friends without quite deceiving your enemies." With respect to Iraq, Cornford was probably a little too optimistic. The degree of credulity given to the Bush administration's rhetoric can be mapped in a series of concentric circles emanating from Washington, D.C. The Washington opinion makers in their think tanks, lobby shops, and bureaucracies are the people who have come to believe in their own propaganda with the greatest passion and the least ability to absorb nuance and criticism. The rest of the United States constitutes the next circle of credulity. Outside Washington, many Americans were initially persuaded to believe the case for war, but that belief has steadily eroded. And simply setting foot outside the borders of the United States into either Canada or Mexico will take you into territory where the public has consistently and strongly opposed the war since its inception.[12]

Fan out farther, and the skepticism increases. On the eve of the war with Iraq, the invasion was opposed by 85 percent of the people of Spain, 86 percent of Germans, 91 percent of Russians. In the Middle East, the White House message on Iraq was accepted by less than 10 percent of the population. A March 2003 survey by the Pew Research Center for People and the Press found that in the year leading up to the war, the percentage of people in France who held a favorable view of the United States dropped from 63 percent to 31 percent. In Italy, it fell from 70 to 34; in Russia, from 61 to 28; in Turkey, from 30 to 12. Even in the United Kingdom, only 48 percent of the population held a favorable view of the United States, down from 75 percent the previous year.[13] A year after the invasion, another Pew survey found that "discontent with America and its policies has intensified rather than diminished. Opinion of the United States in France and Germany is at least as negative now as at the war's conclusion, and British views are decidedly more critical. Perceptions of American unilateralism remain widespread in European and Muslim nations, and the war in Iraq has undermined America's credibility abroad. Doubts about the motives behind the U.S.-led war on terrorism abound, and a growing percentage of Europeans want foreign policy and security arrangements independent from the United States."[14] In 2005, a survey of six Arab countries by the polling firm of Zogby International found strongly negative views of the United States in every country, with only 9 percent of Saudi Arabians and 14 percent of Egyptians expressing a favorable view.[15]

While White House efforts at "public diplomacy" regarding Iraq failed miserably to influence opinions beyond the borders of the United States, the spin did achieve one victory. It enforced a remarkable consistency of rhetoric and thought within the administration itself. The White House plotted public appearances by top officials on a daily "communications grid," making sure that an administration official gave a news briefing every two hours, and that officials all said the same thing. The phrase "death squads" was chosen as the term with which to describe Saddam Hussein's military forces. The word "regime" was chosen whenever his government was mentioned. Republican adviser Frank Luntz circulated a memo recommending that GOP politicians avoid the word "preemption" and the phrase "war in Iraq" when talking about the Bush administration's preemptive war in Iraq. Rather than "preemption," he suggested, "Your efforts are about 'the principles of prevention and protection' in the greater 'War on Terror.' . . . If you describe it simply as 'preemptive action,' some Americans will carry deep reservations about the rightness of the cause. Americans are conditioned to think that hitting first is usually wrong." The willful self-blinding in such documents is hard to parody. As Luntz laid out language to obscure the reality of a unilaterally declared war, he also talked loftily about "ending the Culture of Hate," and declared, "We need to tell leaders from these countries that violence as a means to a political end is unacceptable"—as though the war in Iraq were not itself a prime example of "violence as a means to a political end."[16]

As the invasion of Iraq turned into an occupation, the linguistic spin-doctoring continued. At Fort Bragg, North Carolina, soldiers preparing for deployment to Iraq received training in how to talk to journalists, and were issued plastic laminated cards with such talking points as "We are not an occupying force."[17] Military and political leaders also struggled to find the best-sounding term to describe the insurgency. At first the insurgents were called "dead-enders" or "Baathist holdouts." When the insurgency turned out to be widespread, noted Michael Keane in the *Los Angeles Times*, "its members were 'former regime loyalists.' Then, when it was pointed out that 'loyalty' generally has a positive connotation, the term mutated to 'former regime elements.'"[18]

Great Expectations

Winston Churchill, in his first speech to the British House of Commons as prime minister during World War II, invoked the goal of "victory" using language that might at first blush seem similar to the language used by President Bush in his speech to naval cadets. Churchill called for "Victory at all costs, victory in spite of all terror, victory, however long and hard the road may be; for without victory, there is no survival." The difference, though, is that Churchill spoke at a time when there was little doubt that the nation was indeed facing a stark choice between victory and survival. The war in Iraq, by contrast, was a war of choice. And Churchill made no effort to hide or minimize the price of war. "I have nothing to offer but blood, toil, tears, and sweat," he told his audience. "We have before us an ordeal of the most grievous kind. We have before us many, many long months of struggle and of suffering."

There is no human enterprise more full of danger than waging war, and any nation that considers doing so ought to begin with a careful, sober appraisal of the worst possible outcomes. In preparing for the war in Iraq, however, White House and Pentagon planners based their plans on optimistic, best-case rather than worst-case scenarios. They assumed that Iraqis would joyously welcome U.S. and international troops as liberators, that it would be easy to replace Saddam Hussein's regime with a new, democratic state, and that a long-term war of occupation would not be necessary.

At the onset of war, White House officials confidently predicted that Iraq's vast oil wealth could finance its own postwar reconstruction. In testimony before Congress on March 27, 2003, just days after the invasion of Iraq began, Deputy Secretary of Defense Paul Wolfowitz said, "The oil revenues of that country could bring between 50 and 100 billion dollars over the course of the next two or three years. . . . We are dealing with a country that can really finance its own reconstruction and relatively soon."[19] Writing in the *San Francisco Chronicle*, reporter Robert Collier predicted that "the world's biggest oil bonanza in recent memory may be just around the corner, giving U.S. oil companies huge profits and American consumers cheap gasoline for decades to come. And it all may come courtesy of a war with Iraq." Citing pro-war think tanks such as the American Enterprise Institute, Collier wrote that "a new Iraq oil boom could begin within two years of the war's end. . . . Once production reaches its full capacity, they say, the enormous increase in supply could weaken OPEC, the oil producers' cartel led by Saudi Arabia, lower international oil prices for the foreseeable future and shift the balance of power among the world's major oil producers."[20]

But as Bush delivered his "plan for victory" speech two and a half years later, Iraq's oil production continued to lag behind prewar levels. On the eve of war in March 2003, Iraq was producing 2.5 million barrels of oil per day. Once the war began, production fell off sharply, and two years later, it had only recovered to the level of 2 million barrels per day. During 2005, production declined further as a result of repeated sabotage from insurgents combined with poor project management and political instability. By November 2005, production had fallen to 1.2 million barrels per day, and in December it averaged 1.1 — the lowest level since the war began.[21] What oil revenues existed were drained away by government corruption, security problems, and other pressing claims on the country's resources, leaving nothing for reconstruction. By August 2003, the occupation of Iraq was costing the U.S. $1 billion per week, contributing to the largest federal deficit in American history.[22] By the end of 2005, the war was costing $5.9 billion per month.[23] According to a study released in 2006 by Nobel Prize–winning economist Joseph Stiglitz, the real cost to the United States of the war in Iraq will be $1 to $2 trillion after considering factors such as higher oil prices due to the war and lifetime disabilities and health care for wounded soldiers.[24]

Wolfowitz's rosy prediction about the economic cost of war has turned out to be one of many examples of pro-war optimism that proved to be mirages once put to the test of reality:

➤ Shortly before the war began, the White House rejected the advice of Army Chief of Staff Eric Shinseki, who told the Senate Armed Forces Committee that "something on the order of several hundred thousand soldiers" would be necessary to maintain order in Iraq after Saddam Hussein was toppled. "We're talking about post-hostilities control over a piece of geography that's fairly significant, with the kinds of ethnic tensions that could lead to other problems," Shinseki warned.[25] U.S. Defense Secretary Donald Rumsfeld dismissed this estimate as "off the mark," and Wolfowitz told a congressional hearing that it was *wildly* off the mark," because Iraqi civilians "will greet us as liberators, and that will help us to keep requirements down."[26]

➤ On August 8, 2003, the White House issued a report titled *Results in Iraq: 100 Days Toward Security and Freedom,* which purported to offer one hundred points of progress since the fall of Baghdad: ten "ways the liberation of Iraq supports the war on terror," ten "signs of better security," and so forth. As an example of progress against terrorism, the report stated that the war had destroyed a "safe haven" for "senior al Qaida associate Abu Musab al-Zarqawi," who "came to Baghdad in May 2002 for medical treatment."[27] A year later, a CIA assessment concluded that there was no collaborative relationship between Iraq and Al Qaeda, and no evidence that Saddam Hussein even knew Zarqawi was in Baghdad during his reported visit there in 2002.[28] After the fall of Saddam, however, Zarqawi's terrorist career flourished. Eleven days after the White House issued *100 Days Toward Security and Freedom,* Zarqawi was linked to the Canal Hotel bombing of United Nations headquarters, which prompted the UN to withdraw some six hundred of its international staff from Baghdad, along with employees of other aid agencies. U.S. officials now credit Zarqawi with killing more than seven hundred people under their watch, mostly through terrorist bombings.

➤ In September 2003, Bush administration officials cited opinion polls which they said showed that Iraqis had a positive view of the U.S. occupation. By a two-to-one margin, the poll by Gallup showed that Iraqis thought getting rid of Saddam Hussein was worth the hardships they had endured. However, the White House failed to mention that the same polls also showed that only 33 percent of Iraqis thought they were better off than before the occupation, while 47 percent said they were worse off, and 94 percent said Baghdad was a more dangerous place to live. Only 29 percent of Baghdad residents had a favorable view of the U.S., while 44 percent had a negative view. By comparison, 55 percent had a favorable view of France.[29]

Negatory News

As conditions deteriorated in Iraq, U.S. officials continued to accentuate the positive, pointing to schools that had reopened, the arrival of new fire trucks in Baghdad, electricity returning, water pumps repaired. The news media, they complained, told only the bad news and ignored the good. By September of 2004, however, the U.S. Agency for International Development (USAID) was getting reports from Kroll, one of its security contractors, describing a broad and intensifying campaign of daily attacks by insurgents. After the Kroll reports found their way into the *Washington Post*, USAID restricted distribution of further reports "to those who need it for security planning in Iraq."[30]

As for the supposed gap between reality and news reports, journalists have actually underplayed rather than overplayed the negative. Following the invasion phase of the war, researchers at George Washington University analyzed 1,820 stories on five American networks: ABC, CBS, NBC, CNN, and Fox News as well as the Arab satellite channel Al Jazeera. They found that "all of the American media largely shied away from showing visuals of coalition, Iraqi military, or civilian casualties. Despite advanced technologies offering reporters the chance to transmit the reality of war in real time, reporters chose instead to present a largely bloodless conflict to viewers, even when they did broadcast during firefights. . . . For American viewers in particular, the portrait of war offered by the networks was a sanitized one free of bloodshed, dissent, and diplomacy but full of exciting weaponry, splashy graphics, and heroic soldiers."[31]

Newspaper coverage during the subsequent occupation has also been sanitized. In May 2005, *Los Angeles Times* writer James Rainey reviewed the coverage of six prominent U.S. newspapers (his own included) and the nation's two most popular newsmagazines during a six-month period when 559 Americans and Western allies died. "Despite the considerable bloodshed during that half-year," he reported, "readers of the *Atlanta*

Journal-Constitution, Los Angeles Times, New York Times, St. Louis Post-Dispatch, and *Washington Post* did not see a single picture of a dead serviceman. The *Seattle Times* ran a photo three days before Christmas of the covered body of a soldier killed in the mess hall bombing. Neither *Time* nor *Newsweek,* the weekly newsmagazines, showed any U.S. battlefield dead during that time." Rainey interviewed photojournalists and editors who offered a number of explanations for the lack of coverage: "With a relative handful of photographers at any time covering a nation the size of California, a probing camera is usually absent when a guerrilla attack erupts. . . . Photojournalists sometimes withhold the most striking images from Iraq on their own." In addition, editors who ran photos that showed the horrors of war were "hammered" by "conservative Internet commentators" or faced complaints from pro-war readers who called them "cruel, insensitive, even unpatriotic."[32]

Another reason for limited news coverage from Iraq is that conditions have gotten so bad that reporters find it increasingly difficult to work there at all. In 2004, Farnaz Fassihi, the *Wall Street Journal*'s Baghdad correspondent, sent an e-mail to friends back home that was not intended for publication. It leaked out anyway, giving a vivid description of the difficulties she faced as a journalist:

Being a foreign correspondent in Baghdad these days is like being under virtual house arrest. . . . I am house bound. I leave when I have a very good reason to and a scheduled interview. I avoid going to people's homes and never walk in the streets. I can't go grocery shopping anymore, can't eat in restaurants, can't strike a conversation with strangers, can't look for stories, can't drive in anything but a full armored car, can't go to scenes of breaking news stories, can't be stuck in traffic, can't speak English outside, can't take a road trip, can't say I'm an American, can't linger at checkpoints, can't be curious about what people are saying, doing, feeling. And can't and can't. There has been one too many close calls, including a car bomb so near our house that it blew out all the windows. So now my most pressing concern every day is not to write a kick-ass story but to stay alive and make sure our Iraqi employees stay alive. In Baghdad I am a security personnel first, a reporter second.

Fassihi's letter also offered a more candid assessment of the overall situation in Iraq than most actual news reports:

... the Iraqi government doesn't control most Iraqi cities, there are several car bombs going off each day around the country killing and injuring scores of innocent people, the country's roads are becoming impassable and littered by hundreds of landmines and explosive devices aimed to kill American soldiers, there are assassinations, kidnappings and beheadings. The situation, basically, means a raging barbaric guerilla war. In four days, 110 people died and over 300 got injured in Baghdad alone. . . . Insurgents now attack Americans 87 times a day. . . .

One could argue that Iraq is already lost beyond salvation. For those of us on the ground it's hard to imagine what if anything could salvage it from its violent downward spiral. The genie of terrorism, chaos and mayhem has been unleashed onto this country as a result of American mistakes, and it can't be put back into a bottle.[33]

Fassihi's friends forwarded her e-mail to others, and soon it was circulating widely, creating what her editor called a "sensitive situation." Some journalists said the public attention given to her e-mail would undercut her credibility as a reporter and suggested that maybe she should be reassigned to cover something other than Iraq—even though other reporters in Iraq said her assessment hit the mark. According to *New York Times* reporter Alex Berenson, Fassihi's e-mail was "entirely accurate in its description of reporting conditions. . . . What good news are we supposed to be reporting when the murder rate in Baghdad has gone up 20-fold or more since we entered the city last year, and when we can't even walk the streets?"[34]

The Spin War at Home

The danger of negative news, according to President Bush, is that it may undermine morale and support for the war, as Americans "look at the violence they see each night on their television screens and they wonder how I can remain so optimistic about the prospects of success in Iraq."[35] But propaganda itself is a danger to the nation, as the United States has long recognized, both in theory and in law. In 1948, Congress, concerned by what it had seen propaganda do to Hitler's Germany, passed the Smith-Mundt Act, a law that forbids domestic dissemination of

U.S. government materials intended for foreign audiences. The law is so strict that programming from Voice of America, the government's overseas news service, may not be broadcast to domestic audiences. Legislators were concerned that giving any U.S. administration access to the government's tools for influencing opinion overseas would undermine the democratic process at home. Since 1951, this concern has also been expressed in the appropriations acts passed each year by Congress, which include language that stipulates, "No part of any appropriation contained in this or any other Act shall be used for publicity or propaganda purposes within the United States not heretofore authorized by Congress."

Economic and media globalization, however, have shrunk the planet in ways that blur the distinction between foreign and domestic propaganda. This has been acknowledged in the U.S. Defense Department's *Information Operations Roadmap*, a seventy-four-page document approved in 2003 by Donald Rumsfeld. It noted that "information intended for foreign audiences, including public diplomacy and PSYOP [psychological operations], increasingly is consumed by our domestic audience and vice-versa. PSYOP messages disseminated to any audience . . . will often be replayed by the news media for much larger audiences, including the American public."[36] This ought to be of particular concern to Americans because the Pentagon's doctrine for psychological operations specifically contemplates "actions to convey and (or) deny selected information and indicators to foreign audiences to influence their emotions, motives, and objective reasoning. . . . In various ways, perception management combines truth projection, operations security, cover, and deception, and psyops."[37]

An example of a psyops operation that used "deception" in Iraq occurred during the 2004 preparations for the U.S. military assault on Fallujah, which had become a stronghold for insurgents. On October 14, a spokesman for the marines appeared on CNN and announced that the long-awaited military campaign to retake Fallujah had begun. In fact, the announcement was a deliberate falsehood. The announcement on CNN was intended to trick the insurgents so that U.S. commanders could see how they would react to the real offensive, which would not begin until three weeks later. In giving this bit of false information to CNN, however, the marines were not merely reaching a "foreign audience" but also Americans who watch CNN.[38]

Much of the U.S. propaganda effort, however, is aimed not at tactical deception of enemy combatants but at influencing morale and support for the war in the United States. The Office of Media Outreach, a taxpayer-funded arm of the Department of Defense, has offered government-subsidized trips to Iraq for radio talk-show hosts. "Virtually all expenses are being picked up by the U.S. government, with the exception of broadcasters providing their own means of broadcasting or delivering their content," reported *Billboard* magazine's Radio Monitor website.[39] Office of Media Outreach activities included hosting "Operation Truth," a one-week tour of Iraq by right-wing talk-show hosts, organized by Russo Marsh & Rogers, a Republican PR firm based in California that sponsors a conservative advocacy group called Move America Forward. The purpose of the "Truth Tour," they reported on the Move America Forward website, was "to report the good news on Operation Iraqi Freedom you're not hearing from the old line news media . . . to get the news straight from our troops serving in Operation Iraqi Freedom, including the positive developments and successes they are achieving."[40] Even before the trip began, however, the radio talkers' take on Iraq was already decided. "The war is being won, if not already won, I think," said tour participant Buzz Patterson in a predeparture interview with Fox News. "[Iraq] is stabilized and we want the soldiers themselves to tell the story."[41]

In September 2004, the U.S. military circulated a request for proposals, inviting private public relations firms to apply for a contract to perform an "aggressive" PR and advertising push inside Iraq to include weekly reports on Iraqi public opinion, production of news releases, video news, the training of Iraqis to serve as spokesmen, and creation of a "rebuttal cell" that would monitor all media throughout Iraq, "immediately and effectively responding to reports that unfairly target the Coalition or Coalition interests."[42] According to the request for proposals, "Recent polls suggest support for the Coalition is falling and more and more Iraqis are questioning Coalition resolve, intentions, and effectiveness. It is essential to the success of the Coalition and the future of Iraq that the Coalition gain widespread Iraqi acceptance of its core themes and messages."[43]

The contract, valued initially at $5.4 million, went to Iraqex, a newly formed company based in Washington, D.C., that was set up specifically to provide services in Iraq. Not long thereafter, Iraqex changed its name to the Lincoln Group. Its success in winning the contract "is something of a mystery," the *New York Times* would report a year later, since the "two men who ran the small business had no background in public relations or the media."[44] They were: Christian Bailey, a thirty-year-old businessman from England, and Paige Craig, a thirty-one-year-old former marine intelligence officer. Before taking the PR job in Iraq, they had racked up a string of short-lived businesses such as Express Action, an Internet-based shipping company that raised $14 million in startup financing during the dot-com boom but disappeared within two years; or Motion Power, an attempt to invent a shoe that would generate electrical power.[45] Bailey had also been active with Lead21, a fund-raising and networking operation for young Republicans. Shortly before the commencement of war in Iraq, he set up shop in Iraq, offering "tailored intelligence services" for "government clients faced with critical intelligence challenges." In its various incarnations, Iraqex/Lincoln dabbled in real estate, published a short-lived online business publication called the *Iraq Business Journal*, and tried its hand at exporting scrap metal, manufacturing construction materials, and providing logistics for U.S. forces before finally striking gold with the Pentagon PR contract.

Lincoln partnered initially with the Rendon Group, a public relations firm that had already played a major role in leading the U.S. into war through its work for Ahmed Chalabi and his Iraqi National Congress. (For details, see chapter four.) A few weeks later, Rendon dropped out of the project and left Lincoln in charge. Lincoln hired another Washington-based public relations firm as a subcontractor—BKSH & Associates, headed by Republican political strategist Charles R. Black, Jr. BKSH is a subsidiary of Burson-Marsteller, a PR firm whose previous experience in Iraq also included work for Chalabi and the Iraqi National Congress. Other Pentagon contracts for public relations work were awarded to SYColeman Inc. of Arlington, Virginia, and Science Applications International Corporation. All totaled, the PR contracts added up to $300 million over a five-year period.[46]

On November 30, 2005—the same day that Bush gave his "Plan for Victory" speech to naval cadets—taxpayers got their first glimpse at what was being done with their money. The *Los Angeles Times* reported that the U.S. military was "secretly paying Iraqi newspapers to publish stories written by American troops in an effort to burnish the image of the U.S. mission in Iraq. The articles, written by U.S. military 'information operations' troops, are translated into Arabic and placed in Baghdad newspapers."[47] In an effort to mask any connection with the military, the Pentagon had employed the Lincoln Group to translate and place the stories. When delivering the stories to media outlets in Baghdad, Lincoln's staff and subcontractors had sometimes posed as freelance reporters or advertising executives. The amounts paid ranged from $50 to $2,000 per story placed.[48] All told, the Lincoln Group had planted more than one thousand stories in the Iraqi and Arab press.[49]

The U.S. Army also went directly into the journalism business itself, launching a publication called *Baghdad Now*, with articles written by some of its Iraqi translators, who received training in journalism from a sergeant in the First Armored Division's

Public Affairs Office.[50] The U.S. also founded and financed the Baghdad Press Club, ostensibly a gathering place for Iraqi journalists. In December 2005, however, it was revealed that the military had also been using the press club to pay journalists for writing stories favorable to the U.S. and the occupation. For each story they wrote and placed in an Iraqi newspaper, they received $25, or $45 if the story ran with photos.[51]

The planted stories were "basically factual," U.S. officials told the *Los Angeles Times*, although they admitted that they presented only one side of events and omitted information that might reflect poorly on the U.S. or Iraqi governments. Actually, though, concealing the fact that the stories were written and paid for by the United States was itself a form of deception. Concealment of sponsorship, in fact, is the very standard by which the U.S. Government Accountability Office *defines* propaganda. In a 1988 report that has served as a standard ever since, the GAO stated, "Our decisions have defined covert propaganda as materials such as editorials or other articles prepared by an agency or its contractors at the behest of the agency and circulated as the ostensible position of parties outside the agency. . . . A critical element of covert propaganda is the concealment of the agency's role in sponsoring such material."[52]

"In the very process of preventing misinformation from another side, they are creating misinformation through a process that disguises the source for information that is going out," said John J. Schulz, the dean of Boston University's College of Communications. "You can't be creating a model for democracy while subverting one of its core principles, a free independent press."[53]

When the program was exposed, government officials responded with contradictory statements. The White House denied any knowledge of the program, and Donald Rumsfeld said at first that it was "troubling." General Peter Pace, chairman of the Joint Chiefs of Staff, said he was "concerned." In Iraq, however, a military spokesman said the program was "an important part of countering misinformation in the news by insurgents."[54] A couple of months later, Rumsfeld claimed that the pay-for-praise operation had been shut down. "When we heard about it, we said, 'Gee, that's not what we ought to be doing' and told the people down there. . . . They stopped doing that," Rumsfeld told interviewer Charlie Rose during an appearance on public television. However, he said, "It wasn't anything terrible that happened," and he argued that U.S. media exposure of the program was unfortunate because it would have a "chilling effect" on "anyone involved in public affairs in the military," preventing them from doing "anything that the media thinks is not exactly the way we do it in America."[55] The problem, in other words, was not that the United States was running a covert propaganda operation. The problem was that there were still independent journalists in the United States capable of straying from the script. Even more unfortunately for Rumsfeld, those same journalists happened to notice that he was not telling the truth when he said the program had been shut down. Four days after his interview with Charlie Rose, Rumsfeld was forced to admit that he had been "mistaken" and that the program was merely "under review."[56] A couple of weeks later General George Casey, the top U.S. commander in Iraq, said the military's review had found that it was acting "within our authorities and responsibilities" in paying to place stories in the press, and that it had no plans to stop.[57]

It is difficult to imagine that Rumsfeld and other White House officials were as naive as they pretended to be when they denied knowledge of the Lincoln Group's activities, since Lincoln's work was closely coordinated with the Pentagon's psychological operations unit, a 1,200-person organization based in Fort Bragg, North Carolina, whose media center was so large that the *New York Times* called it "the envy of any global communications company."[58] The Pentagon had spent $57.6 million on contracts to the Rendon Group and Lincoln Group—an amount that "is more than the annual newsroom budget allotted to most American newsrooms *to cover all the news from everywhere for an entire year*," observed Paul McLeary, a politics and media reporter for the *Columbia Journalism Review.* Spending on that scale, he added, "sure sounds like well-financed policy to us—and a well-coordinated one as well—and not one hatched by low-level officials who never let their bosses at the White House in on what they were doing."[59]

Interviews with Lincoln Group employees also undercut the claim that their work was some kind of rogue operation. "In clandestine parlance, Lincoln Group was a 'cutout'—a third party—that would provide the military with plausible deniability," said a former Lincoln Group employee in an interview with the *Los Angeles Times.* "To attribute products to [the military] would defeat the entire purpose," he said. "Hence, no product by Lincoln Group ever said 'Made in the U.S.A.' "

Another former Lincoln employee openly scoffed at the program on grounds that it was having no effect on Iraqi public opinion: "In my own estimation, this stuff has absolutely no effect, and it's a total waste of money. Every Iraqi can read right through it."[60]

The question, then, is who *was* believing it? Just who was the United States really fooling? The answer is that it was mostly fooling itself.

CHAPTER TWO

The Plame Game

"**NEARLY ALL MEN CAN STAND ADVERSITY,**" **LINCOLN** said, "but if you want to test a man's character, give him power." President Bush went to war in Iraq at a time when he held more power than any other American president in recent memory. For the first time in decades, the midterm elections of 2002 had given the Republican Party clear majorities in both houses of Congress at the same time that Bush held the White House. Moreover, Bush's party was united internally, while the Democrats were divided. Fearful of seeming soft on national security, half of the Democrats in Congress had voted for a resolution authorizing Bush to go to war.

Adversity tests what someone will do when desperate, but the test of power tells us what people will do when they think they can act with impunity. We can therefore learn a great deal from examining how a conflict between the Bush administration and its critics led to the exposure of Valerie Plame Wilson as a covert agent for the Central Intelligence Agency. The incident tells us what the White House thought it could get away with in terms of manipulation of truth and punishing disagreement. It also tells us something about the fleeting nature of power. At its beginning, the "Plamegate" affair seemed to be a quibble about a minor detail in the Bush administration's case for war — specifically, the question of whether Bush was correct when he claimed that Saddam Hussein's regime had been seeking to purchase uranium in Africa. The White House, seemingly invincible at that moment, could have easily conceded its error on this point without substantially affecting the rhetorical force of the rest of its argument. Instead, it chose to attack, with consequences that proved devastating for the White House itself.

Opinion pollsters have frequently noted a tendency for presidential approval ratings to shoot upward during wars and other international crises — something they call the "rally around the flag effect." At moments of crisis, people tend to put aside their political differences to "support the president" and "support the troops." Perhaps no president in history has benefited from the rally effect as much as George W. Bush. Immediately following the September 11, 2001, terrorist attacks, his popularity shot up to 90 percent — the highest rating recorded for any president since the Gallup polling organization began collecting data in the days of Franklin Delano Roosevelt. (Roosevelt himself topped out at 84 percent following the Japanese attack on Pearl Harbor, and Bush's father reached 89 percent during Operation Desert Storm.)[1] By the end of 2002, Bush's popularity had declined to roughly the level it was at before 9/11, but with the beginning of the war in Iraq, it rose again to 71 percent.

Eventually, however, the rally effect fades. Bush's popularity began to decline again almost as soon as the government of Saddam Hussein collapsed. Perhaps Americans were beginning to realize that the invasion phase of the war was only the prelude to a much longer war of occupation. Between April and July 2003, the number of Americans who believed that the United States was in control in Iraq fell from 71 percent to 45 percent, while the number of those who believed the Bush administration had overstated the threat from Iraq's weapons rose from 44 to 56 percent.[2] During that same time period, Bush's presidential approval ratings saw the sharpest three-month decline of his entire presidency, falling from 64.0 to 55.7 percent and bringing the administration perilously close to the tipping point at which a president goes from being liked to being disliked by a majority of the public.[3]

One event in particular seems to have contributed strongly to Bush's decline: the revelation that he relied on faulty information in his January 28, 2003, State of the Union address. "The British government has learned that Saddam Hussein recently sought significant quantities of uranium from Africa," Bush said, a sixteen-word sentence that has since become infamous.[4]

At the time Bush said those words, they seemed to clinch his case that Iraq was on the verge of becoming a nuclear threat. Subsequently, however, the White House was forced to admit that this claim was based on forged documents—forgeries that were so obviously fake that they astonished experts who examined them. According to an official with the International Atomic Energy Agency (IAEA), which exposed the forgeries, "These documents are so bad that I cannot imagine that they came from a serious intelligence agency."[5]

The public unraveling of the forgeries happened to occur during the period when our previous book about the war in Iraq, *Weapons of Mass Deception*, arrived in bookstores. In *Weapons of Mass Deception*, we wrote about the Bush administration's unusual commitment to "message discipline"—the public relations art of coordinating statements by administration officials to ensure that they conform to the administration's planned talking points. We watched with some surprise, therefore, as the Bush team spent several weeks floundering in search of a response to accusations that it had knowingly used false information or, at best, had cherry-picked evidence to make the case for war. In this case, message discipline seems to have failed them badly. What might have been a minor footnote to history became instead a major scandal, sparking a criminal investigation and the indictment of I. Lewis "Scooter" Libby, the chief of staff to Vice President Dick Cheney, on charges of lying to a grand jury.

Follow the Yellowcake Road

Some of the details surrounding the origins of the forged documents remain unclear, but it is now known that they came from Rocco Martino, an Italian businessman who has made a career out of selling information to intelligence agencies. In 1999, an Iraqi ambassador made a public visit to Niger and two other African countries, and although the stated purpose of the visit was routine, Martino became aware that French officials suspected Iraq might have a hidden motive. Niger produces uranium oxide, also known as "yellowcake," a raw material used in the manufacture of nuclear reactor fuel rods, and the French wondered if Iraq might be trying to obtain some. Through his contacts with a woman who worked at Niger's embassy in Rome, Martino obtained documents that seemed to support this suspicion. Reports based on Martino's information were prepared by Italy's military intelligence agency, the Servizio per le Informazioni e la Sicurezza Militare (SISMI), as well as by the British spy agency MI6. In the wake of the 9/11 terrorist attacks, this information was passed to U.S. intelligence analysts.

Early on, however, serious questions emerged about the reliability of these reports. For starters, they talked about a deal to divert *500 tons* of uranium ore from Niger to Iraq—one sixth of Niger's total annual production. On November 20, 2001, the U.S. Embassy in Niger reported hearing from the head of Niger's French-owned mining consortium, who said "there was no possibility" of such a diversion. A U.S. State Department analyst agreed that Iraq was unlikely to risk a transaction on that scale because it was "bound to be caught."[6] At the request of the United States, French intelligence agents conducted their own separate investigation and reached the same conclusions. The French had seen Martino's documents and had determined that they were forged. Even so, they sent a team to Niger to double-check any reports of a sale or an attempt to purchase uranium.

The team found nothing, and reported their findings back to the CIA. In the words of French intelligence official Alain Chouet, "We told the Americans, 'Bullshit. It doesn't make any sense.'"[7]

Barbro Owens-Kirkpatrick, the U.S. ambassador to Niger, also investigated the story and concluded that it was unfounded. General Carlton Fulford, Jr., the deputy commander in charge of U.S. armed forces in Europe, visited Niger in February 2002 to investigate the Iraq-Niger story and returned satisfied that there was nothing to it.[8] The CIA also dispatched Joseph C. Wilson IV, a former ambassador with experience and contacts in both Niger and Iraq, to make his own visit and investigate.

Wilson had considerable reason to mistrust Saddam Hussein's intentions. From 1988 to 1991, he served as deputy chief of mission at the U.S. Embassy in Baghdad. April Glaspie, the ambassador, was out of the country on vacation when Iraq invaded Kuwait, and she never returned. During the five following months that led up to Operation Desert Storm, Wilson served as acting ambassador, a role he performed with considerable audacity. At one press conference in Baghdad, he showed up wearing a hangman's noose around his neck to dramatize his scorn for the brutality of Saddam's regime, which was trying to take American citizens hostage in an attempt to blackmail the United States out of going to war. "If he wants to execute me for keeping Americans from being taken hostage, I will bring my own fucking rope," Wilson declared.[9] His willingness to confront the regime prompted a cable of appreciation from President George H. W. Bush: "What you are doing day in and day out under the most trying conditions is truly inspiring."[10]

When Wilson visited Niger to investigate the yellowcake

claim in February 2002, he held dozens of meetings with current and former government officials as well as people associated with the country's uranium business. His investigation reached the same conclusion that others had reached previously: "Given the structure of the consortiums that operated the mines, it would be exceedingly difficult for Niger to transfer uranium to Iraq. Niger's uranium business consists of two mines, Somair and Cominak, which are run by French, Spanish, Japanese, German and Nigerian interests. If the government wanted to remove uranium from a mine, it would have to notify the consortium, which in turn is strictly monitored by the International Atomic Energy Agency. Moreover, because the two mines are closely regulated, quasi-governmental entities selling uranium would require the approval of the minister of mines, the prime minister and probably the president. In short, there's simply too much oversight over too small an industry for a sale to have transpired."[11]

Based on these investigations, the U.S. State Department's Bureau of Intelligence and Research (INR) produced an analysis on March 4, 2002, titled *Niger-Iraq: Sale of Niger Uranium to Iraq Unlikely*. It noted that for Niger to ship five hundred tons of uranium ore would mean that "25 hard-to-conceal 10-ton tractor-trailers would be used to transport the concealed uranium. Because Niger is landlocked the convoy would have to cross at least one international border and would have to travel at least 1,000 miles to reach the sea. Moving such a quantity secretly over such a distance would be very difficult, particularly because the French would be indisposed to approve or cloak this arrangement."[12]

The INR received copies of Rocco Martino's documents in October 2002, and as soon as they were examined by the INR, the analyst concluded that they were fakes. In e-mail to other intelligence agency colleagues, the analyst called the documents "funky," a "hoax," and "obviously a forgery." He noted that the documents included a purported description of some sort of military campaign against major world powers being planned by both Iran and Iraq and orchestrated through Niger's embassy in Rome, which struck the analyst as "completely implausible."[13]

Notwithstanding these reports, the claim that Iraq was seeking uranium from Africa continued to appear in government reports and public statements. In September 2002, the Department of Defense published an assessment titled *Iraq's Reemerging Nuclear Program*, which stated, "Iraq has been vigorously trying to procure yellowcake and uranium ore." The British government published a white paper making the same claim on September 24. The U.S. State Department repeated the claim in a December public statement, which elicited an official complaint and response from the government of Niger, insisting that no such transaction had occurred. The charge appeared again in a January 20, 2003, White House report to Congress, followed by another report published for public distribution three days later—the same day that Paul Wolfowitz repeated the charge in a speech before the Council on Foreign Relations in New York. Condoleezza Rice included it in an op-ed for the *New York Times* titled "Why We Know Iraq Is Lying."[14] On January 26, U.S. Secretary of State Colin Powell repeated the charge in a speech before the World Economic Forum in Davos, Switzerland. "Why is Iraq still trying to procure uranium and the special equipment needed to transform it into material for nuclear weapons?" Powell asked.[15] Two days later, Bush delivered his State of the Union address and personally uttered the now-infamous sixteen words.[16]

Sorry About That, Chief

As soon as the yellowcake story was aired publicly, it began to fall apart. The International Atomic Energy Agency is the agency that was responsible for monitoring Iraq's compliance with the ban on nuclear weapons development. In December 2002, when U.S. and British officials first started talking publicly about reports that Iraq was seeking uranium, IAEA officials asked to see the evidence so they could investigate. On January 9, IAEA director general Mohamed ElBaradei noted in a briefing to the United Nations Security Council that he had not received "any specific information" with which to do so.[17] A few days later, he expanded on the point in an interview with *Time* magazine: "I don't want to come to a definitive conclusion yet. I think it's difficult for Iraq to hide a complete nuclear-weapons program. . . . [W]e need to get specifics of when and where. We need actionable information."[18] On the day Bush gave his State of the Union address, ElBaradei appeared on *NewsHour with Jim Lehrer* and expressed greater skepticism still: "In 1998, we neutralized Iraq's nuclear program when we left Iraq," he said, adding that although there were still unanswered questions about chemical or biological weapons, technological means existed to test whether a nuclear program existed. "It's also because in the nuclear area we have a number of sophisticated techniques to be able to detect any radioactivity or nuclear activity. . . . So overall, we haven't seen any evidence of revival of a nuclear weapons program in Iraq." He added that UN nuclear inspectors in Iraq had not yet completed their job, but expressed confidence that "in the next few months, barring exceptional circumstances, we should be able to give you some good credible assurance on the nuclear program."[19]

It took six weeks of asking before the IAEA was finally able to get copies of the Niger documents from the United States. When they finally received them on February 8, it took only a few hours to verify that they were fakes. One letter appeared on an obsolete letterhead that contained the wrong symbol for the presidency and references to government bodies that did not exist at the time it was supposedly written. Another letter, dated October 10, 2000, was signed by Niger's foreign minister, Allele Elhadj Habibou—who had left office in 1989. Worse still, the letter had a date stamp showing that it was received in September 2000—in other words, before it was sent. Another letter, allegedly from the president of Niger, had a signature that had obviously been faked and a text with inaccuracies so egregious that an IEAE official said "they could be spotted by someone using Google on the Internet."[20]

On March 7, 2003—thirteen days before the start of war—ElBaradei reported these findings forcefully and in detail to the United Nations Security Council.[21] In Europe, newspapers were filled with reports that the United States had used fabricated evidence to make the case for war. In the United States news media, however, ElBaradei's findings received only a few brief mentions, and they were dismissed out of hand by Vice President Dick Cheney. "We believe he has, in fact, reconstituted nuclear weapons. I think Mr. ElBaradei frankly is wrong," Cheney said on *Meet the Press*.[22] A senior State Department official blasted the weapons inspectors as "pathetically unaggressive, amateurish and believing everything the Iraqis tell them."[23]

The IAEA revelation came too late to alter the course of events. America was getting ready for war, and Bush's popularity was spiking upward. It did, however, trouble Democratic congressman Henry Waxman, who asked for an explanation in a letter addressed to President Bush. In September of the previous year, Waxman had voted to authorize military action against Iraq—largely, he said, on the basis of the administration's claims about Iraq's nuclear intentions. "Although chemical and biological weapons can inflict casualties, no argument for attacking Iraq is as compelling as the possibility of Saddam Hussein brandishing nuclear bombs," he wrote. "That, obviously, is why the evidence in this area is so crucial, and why so many have looked to you for honest and credible information on Iraq's nuclear capability." The IAEA's revelation, he wrote, raised "troubling questions. It appears that at the same time you, Secretary Rumsfeld and State Department officials were citing Iraq's efforts to obtain uranium from Africa as a crucial part of the case against Iraq, U.S. intelligence officials regarded this very same information as unreliable. If true, this is deeply disturbing."[24]

Joseph Wilson was also doing a slow burn. The day after Bush's State of the Union speech, he says, he telephoned a friend at the State Department to say, "Either you guys have some information that's different from what my trip and the ambassador and everybody else said about Niger, or else you need to do something to correct the record."[25] He received no response. A month later, after Mohamed ElBaradei gave his speech to the United Nations exposing the Niger documents as forgeries, Wilson read a story in the *Washington Post* that quoted an unnamed White House official saying, "We fell for it." This struck him as implausible, since he himself had separately debunked the uranium claim for the government thirteen months earlier. On March 8, Wilson was interviewed on CNN. Without disclosing his role as an envoy to Niger, he said that "this particular case is outrageous. . . . I think it's safe to say that the U.S. government should have or did know that this report was a fake before Dr. El-Baradei mentioned it in his report at the UN yesterday."[26]

In May, Wilson discussed his concerns off the record with *New York Times* columnist Nicholas Kristof. Without identifying Wilson by name, Kristof wrote a column stating that "a former U.S. ambassador to Africa" had investigated and debunked the uranium claim long before the White House began using it to make the case for war.[27] Wilson also spoke with *Washington Post* reporter Walter Pincus, who used it as the basis for a story—again, without mentioning Wilson by name.

On June 8, Condoleezza Rice appeared on *Meet the Press* and attempted again to defend the administration's handling of the yellowcake forgery. "Maybe someone knew down in the bowels of the agency, but no one in our circles knew that there were doubts and suspicions that this might be a forgery," she said.[28] This time, Wilson says, he phoned friends close to people in the Bush administration and warned them that if Rice would not correct the record, he would come forward with what he knew.

On July 6, he did. His op-ed, titled "What I Didn't Find in Africa," was published in the *New York Times*. "Those news stories about that unnamed former envoy who went to Niger? That's me," he wrote. "The vice president's office asked a serious question. I was asked to help formulate the answer. I did so, and I have every confidence that the answer I provided was circulated to the appropriate officials within our government. The question now is how that answer was or was not used by our political leadership. If . . . the information was ignored because it did not fit certain preconceptions about Iraq, then a legitimate argument can be made that we went to war under false pretenses."[29]

Over the next three weeks, White House and CIA officials offered a variety of conflicting answers to questions about how the false information wound up in the president's State of the Union address. Rather than quieting questions, the contradictions in their statements gave the story additional legs and kept reporters asking for a coherent explanation:

➤ Immediately following the publication of Wilson's article, the White House admitted publicly for the first time that it had used flawed intelligence information. "It might in fact be wrong," said a senior White House official.[30] White House spokesman Ari Fleischer admitted that Bush's statement in his State of the Union address "was based and predicated on the yellow cake from Niger," which "did turn out to be a forgery." However, he said, the administration had owned up to the mistake a long time ago: "There is zero, nada, nothing new here."[31]

➤ On July 11, CIA director George Tenet stepped forward to take the blame for the error. "These 16 words should never have been included in the text written for the president," he said.[32] Republican senator Richard Shelby promptly stepped forward to demand that Tenet resign for the "failures of intelligence" that had occurred on his watch. Condoleezza Rice also pointed the finger of blame at Tenet: "I can tell you, if the CIA, the director of Central Intelligence, had said 'Take this out of the speech,' it would have been gone, without question," she told reporters. Behind the scenes, however, anonymous CIA officials complained to reporters that just the opposite was true: Tenet, they said, had tried to warn the White House that the Niger claims were bogus, but the White House wouldn't listen.[33]

➤ The following Sunday, Condoleezza Rice and Donald Rumsfeld made separate appearances on Sunday television talk shows in which they insisted that Bush had not misspoken after all. Bush's statement, they said, was based on a broader body of intelligence that included information from the British government that was *not* based on the Niger forgeries. "The statement that he made was indeed accurate. The British government did say that," Rice told Fox News.[34]

➤ Within days, word leaked out that CIA officials *had* warned the White House to avoid claiming that Iraq was seeking uranium from Africa. Tenet had issued the warning person-ally, in a phone conversation with deputy national security advisor Stephen J. Hadley in early October 2002. The CIA had also put its warning in writing, in memoranda sent to Hadley, Rice, and White House speechwriter Michael Ger-son. When the existence of these memoranda surfaced on July 22, 2003, Hadley stepped forward to take the blame for the sixteen words in the speech and said he had apologized to Bush.[35] He also offered his resignation, which Bush mag-nanimously declined.

➤ Condoleezza Rice then stepped up to take a bite of the blame. "I don't remember seeing the memo," she said. "I feel respon-sible for this. It should not have happened to the president."[36]

➤ After everyone else had fallen on their sword, Bush finally stepped forward himself. "I take personal responsibility for everything I say, of course," he said. "Absolutely."[37] For a while, that seemed to quiet the questions.

The Spy Who Loved Me

At the same time that White House officials struggled publicly to answer Wilson's charges, they were working behind the scenes to discredit him personally. Even before he published his editorial, they were already finding ways to respond. Beginning in late May, officials in the office of Dick Cheney began seeking information about Wilson and his trip to Niger. On June 10,

Marc Grossman, the U.S. undersecretary of state for political affairs, received a memo from the Bureau of Intelligence and Research outlining the details. Most of the INR's memo could be interpreted as hurting rather than helping the administration's case. It noted, for example, that the INR had opposed sending Wilson to Niger in the first place—not because he lacked qualifications, but because even before he went, the State Department had already inquired about and disproved the allegation that Iraq was seeking uranium. In a paragraph that discussed the background to Wilson's trip, however, a detail popped up. The paragraph was marked "(S)" for "Secret"—the standard notation used to indicate that information is classified. It stated that Wilson's wife, Valerie Plame Wilson, worked for WINPAC—Weapons Intelligence, Nonproliferation, and Arms Control, the CIA's unit that conducts intelligence research into other countries' programs involving weapons of mass destruction.[38]

Valerie Wilson—or Valerie Plame, the name by which she would soon become known to the public—was not simply a CIA analyst. She was one of the few operatives to become an NOC—an agent operating under "nonofficial cover." Some spies work under "official cover," assuming positions at a seemingly benign department of their government, such as the diplomatic service. This type of cover helps disguise the nature of their work, but their visible affiliation with the government limits the places they can go and inquiries they can make. Nonofficial cover offers a deeper level of secrecy, but at greater risk and expense. NOC agents have no diplomatic status, so if their identity is discovered while they are working overseas, they can be arrested and imprisoned. Valerie Plame Wilson had worked as an over-

seas NOC for two decades, sometimes posing as an employee of
Brewster Jennings & Associates, a CIA front group set up to give
her cover.

Some of what happened after the White House learned that
Wilson's wife was a spy can be found in the statement of indictment that U.S. special prosecutor Patrick J. Fitzerald prepared
in October 2005 against I. Lewis ("Scooter") Libby, the chief of
staff to Vice President Dick Cheney. On or about June 11 or 12,
it states, Libby "was orally advised by the Undersecretary of
State that Wilson's wife worked for the CIA and that State Department personnel were saying that Wilson's wife was involved
in the organization of his trip." He was also told by Dick Cheney
himself that Wilson's wife worked at WINPAC. According to
Fitzgerald's office, "Libby understood that the Vice President
had learned this information from the CIA."[39]

On June 23—two weeks before Wilson's op-ed appeared in
the *New York Times*—Libby met with Judith Miller, a reporter at
the *Times* whom he knew well through her previous reporting
on Iraq's alleged weapons of mass destruction. Miller had in fact
done as much as, if not more than, any other journalist in the
United States to make the case publicly that Iraq possessed
banned weapons that posed an imminent threat. Libby told her
he was upset at the CIA, which he said was engaged in "selective
leaking" aimed at ensuring that the White House rather than the
CIA would be blamed for the failure to find WMDs. Cheney
didn't know Wilson, he said, and knew nothing about his trip to
Niger. He insisted that the CIA had never given warning that the
Niger information might be bad. "No briefer came in and said,
'You got it wrong, Mr. President,'" he said. Libby then offered a

"selective leak" of his own, telling Miller that Wilson's wife worked at the CIA.[40]

On July 8—two days after Wilson's editorial appeared—Libby and Miller met again. This time Libby was even more emphatic in his insistence that Wilson was small fry who didn't know what he was talking about. CIA director George Tenet had never heard of him either, Libby said. And, he added, expanding upon the point that he had made during their previous conversation, Wilson's wife worked for the CIA, at WINPAC.[41]

The fact that Wilson's wife worked for the CIA became a talking point that Libby and other White House officials brought up repeatedly with reporters:

➤ The earliest such mention seems to have occurred in mid-June, when *Washington Post* reporter Bob Woodward says a White House official (as yet unidentified publicly) "told me Wilson's wife worked for the CIA on weapons of mass destruction as a WMD analyst."[42]

➤ On July 7, Libby told White House press secretary Ari Fleischer that Wilson's wife worked at the CIA, adding that the information was not widely known.

➤ On or about July 10 or 11, Libby spoke with a senior White House official who is described in Libby's indictment papers only as "Official A," but who has been widely reported to be Karl Rove, President Bush's top political adviser.[43] During that conversation, Rove recounted his conversation earlier that week with conservative columnist Robert Novak, in which Rove confirmed to Novak that Wilson's wife worked for the CIA. "Libby was advised by Official A that Novak would be writing a story about Wilson's wife," the indictment states.[44]

➤ Rove also spoke with *Time* magazine correspondent Matt Cooper by telephone on July 11. Speaking on "deep background" (meaning that Cooper was free to use the information but not to identify Rove as the source), he told Cooper that Wilson's wife worked on investigating weapons of mass destruction for the CIA and suggested that she was responsible for sending him to Niger.[45] (He did not mention her name, a detail that White House defenders have subsequently interpreted to mean that disclosing her identity as a covert agent was somehow not illegal.) The following day, Cooper followed up by phoning Libby, who confirmed the information that Rove had previously disclosed.[46]

➤ On July 12, as *Washington Post* reporter Walter Pincus later said, he was interviewing an administration official "who was talking to me confidentially about a matter involving alleged Iraqi nuclear activities," when the administration official (whom Pincus has not identified publicly) "veered off the precise matter we were discussing and told me that the White House had not paid attention to former Ambassador Joseph Wilson's CIA-sponsored February 2002 trip to Niger because it was set up as a boondoggle by his wife, an analyst with the agency working on weapons of mass destruction."[47]

On July 14, Robert Novak published his column, which—as Karl Rove had promised a few days earlier—announced publicly for the first time that Wilson's "wife, Valerie Plame, is an agency operative on weapons of mass destruction. Two senior administration officials told me his wife suggested sending Wilson to Niger to investigate the Italian report."[48]

In the days after Novak's column appeared, White House officials continued to draw attention to Wilson's wife. NBC correspondent Andrea Mitchell said she "heard in the White House that people were touting the Novak column and that that was the real story." Wilson says he got a phone call from Chris Matthews, host of MSNBC's *Hardball*. Matthews told him: "I just got off the phone from Karl Rove, who said your wife was fair game."[49]

Killing the Messenger

The introduction of Valerie Plame Wilson's name into public discourse is a particularly high profile example of the propaganda technique known as "ad hominem argumentation," also called "attacking the messenger." Ad hominem argumentation relies on a logical fallacy: by attacking the person who makes an assertion, it avoids answering the assertion itself. Its basic structure is as follows:

1. A makes claim B.
2. There is something objectionable about A.
3. Therefore claim B is false.

In this case, the thing that was deemed "objectionable" about Joseph Wilson was his wife's identity as a CIA agent involved in research into weapons of mass destruction. It is almost surreal that this particular fact could be construed by the White House as something objectionable. Suppose for a moment that Wilson's wife worked as an accountant or a cook or a tennis pro. Would any of those occupations make his statements regarding Niger more or less credible than the job she actually held?

As a somewhat more subtle elaboration of the ad hominem argument, Wilson's attackers claimed that his trip to Niger was a pointless "boondoggle" because his wife had sent him. The Wilsons and the CIA both dispute this claim, stating that although she proposed his name as a possible envoy to Niger, the actual decision to send him was made by her boss, in consultation with other CIA officials. However, let's suppose for a moment that the decision to send him *was* made by Valerie Plame Wilson. Even if that were true, would it have any bearing on the accuracy of his statements?

As time has gone on, a number of other ad hominem arguments have also been put forward in the effort to discredit Wilson:

➤ Wilson was "a liberal Democrat who was for John Kerry," stated former Republican congressman Newt Gingrich on Fox News.[50]

➤ Wilson was "a pro-Saudi, leftist partisan with an ax to grind," according to a column in the conservative magazine, *National Review*.[51]

➤ Wilson went to an anti-Bush fund-raising concert by Bruce Springsteen.

➤ Wilson was flamboyant, a "has been" trying to get back into the limelight.

➤ Wilson's wife wasn't really a CIA agent; her job there was actually menial. Republican congressman Jack Kingston called her "a glorified secretary."[52] (This particular line of attack is both ad hominem and obviously false. It costs the CIA $500,000 to $1 million to set an agent up with nonofficial cover. That kind of money doesn't get spent on secretaries.)

The case of Joseph Wilson is far from the only example of government officials using leaked information or ad hominem arguments to discredit their critics. Usually, though, leaks stop short of illegality. Revealing the identity of a member of the intelligence community is a serious matter—so serious that in 1982 Congress passed the Intelligence Identities Protection Act, which makes the unauthorized identification of a CIA operative a criminal act punishable by up to ten years in federal prison. On this basis, the CIA contacted the U.S. Department of Justice on July 30, 2003, asking for the FBI to "undertake a criminal investigation" of "a possible violation of criminal law concerning the unauthorized disclosure of classified information."[53] A month later, the investigation began.

Valerie Plame Wilson has maintained a public silence about her work as a covert CIA operative, but Joseph Wilson has been outspoken about its ramifications. The loss of her anonymity, he said, effectively ended her career and may also have put others at risk, compromising "every operation, every relationship, every network with which she had been associated in her entire career."[54]

The additional irony, observed United Press International editor Shaun Waterman, is that Valerie Plame Wilson worked for the CIA "on the very issue the Bush administration says was at the heart of its decision to go to war with Iraq: weapons of mass destruction. . . . Plame's outing, whoever did it, has damaged the very effort the White House said it was pursuing in going to war in the first place. A very important line has been crossed here. The integrity of the policy goals—nonproliferation of weapons of mass destruction—is now seen by at least some in the White House as less important than the integrity of the message—we didn't exaggerate the case against Iraq. . . . The message seems to have trumped everything, even the need to get it right in the war on terror."[55]

Chain Reactions

There is a truism that lies breed more lies. The claim that Iraq was seeking uranium from Africa originated with a deception—forged documents that were accepted as authentic by government officials. The question of who committed the original forgery remains a mystery. Various theories have been put forward: someone in the United States government, the British, the Italians. One theory, cited by journalist Seymour Hersh, is that the forgeries were the work of disaffected CIA insiders who wanted to embarrass the White House. Another theory is that they were the work of a con artist looking to make some money by selling documents that told the government what it wanted to hear. Regardless of where the deception originated, it was embraced by the Bush administration through some combination of credulity and/or dishonesty, combined with an eagerness to sell the war. Later, when the original deception was exposed, White House officials engaged in a misguided and possibly criminal effort at damage control based on character assassination aimed at Joseph Wilson after he blew the whistle. Once White House officials had done so, however, they found themselves compelled to tell further lies as they attempted to distance themselves from their own statements to reporters.

On September 16, 2003, White House press secretary Scott McClellan dismissed the idea that Karl Rove was Novak's anonymous source as "totally ridiculous."[56] On September 29, McClellan repeated the denial, adding, "That is not the way this White House operates. . . . Leaking classified information, particularly of this nature, is a very serious matter. . . . If anyone in this administration was involved in it, they would no longer be in this administration." He added, though, that he had spoken personally to Rove about the matter, and "there's been nothing, absolutely nothing, brought to our attention to suggest any White House involvement."[57]

Bush himself weighed in the following day. "I don't know of anybody in my administration who leaked classified information," he said. "If somebody did leak classified information, I'd like to know it, and we'll take appropriate action. . . . Leaks of classified information are a bad thing . . . and I've spoken out consistently against them and I want to know who the leakers are."[58] White House officials then spent the following year stonewalling the Justice Department investigation.

When Libby was interviewed by FBI special agents in October and November 2003, he told them that he had never discussed Valerie Plame Wilson with *New York Times* reporter Judith Miller, and that he did not even know she was Wilson's wife until he heard about it from NBC's Tim Russert. Unfortunately for his case, the reporters with whom he had spoken kept notes. When Libby and Rove talked to reporters about Joseph Wilson's wife, they insisted on doing so anonymously, and the reporters were reluctant to violate their pledge of confidentiality. Months of subpoenas and legal maneuverings followed, and Judith Miller's refusal to testify landed her in jail for eighty-five days before she obtained a waiver from Libby. Her subsequent testimony and notes, along with corroborating evidence from Russert, *Time* magazine reporter Matthew Cooper, and the *Washington Post*'s Walter Pincus, became the basis for Libby's indictment by a federal grand jury on October 31, 2005. He was charged with five counts of obstruction of justice, making false statements, and perjury.[59]

Final Arguments

The attacks on Joseph Wilson and his wife were only part of the administration's attempt to defend the sixteen words in Bush's State of the Union address. White House officials and pro-war pundits made a couple of other arguments that deserve examination.

Some commentators have claimed that Wilson's trip to Niger actually *confirmed* that Iraq was seeking uranium. The main thrust of Wilson's investigation was aimed at finding out whether Iraq had actually *obtained* uranium ore. He determined that this could not have happened because of existing systems of control, combined with the practical impossibility of shipping large quantities of uranium to Iraq undetected. There is, however, a difference between seeking something and actually obtaining it. During his conversations in Niger, Wilson spoke with Niger's former prime minister, Ibrahim Mayaki, who said that he met with a delegation from Iraq in June 1999 to discuss "expanding commercial relations" between the two countries. Because of the United Nations sanctions against Iraq, Mayaki said, he steered the conversation away from trade issues. Mayaki also said that he thought "commercial relations" might be a way to open the door to buying uranium. In fact, however, the word "uranium" never came up at all during that conversation in 1999. Some analysts, nevertheless, viewed Wilson's report on this conversation—in which uranium was not even discussed—as confirmation that Iraq was seeking uranium. Does this in fact tell us anything at all about Iraq, or is it merely an example of evidence being stretched to fit a predetermined conclusion?[60]

White House officials also pointed out that Bush's State of the Union speech never mentioned Niger specifically and claimed that it was based on intelligence reports from England as well as the forged Niger documents. The British have indeed claimed that they had additional information showing that Iraq was seeking uranium from elsewhere in Africa, besides Niger. The official British word on this point can be found in a document called the *Butler Report* after its lead author, Robin Butler, a retired civil servant and member of the British House of Lords. It includes a single sentence, which states that in addition to Niger, British intelligence had "further and separate intelligence" of Iraqi efforts to buy uranium from the Democratic Republic of Congo.[61] However, the *Butler Report* offers no details—not even an approximate date when this may have happened, thus giving no way to assess its credibility. The British have also declined to share any information about this intelligence, even with the International Atomic Energy Agency, which was responsible for prewar monitoring of Iraq's nuclear capability. In any case, the Congo's uranium mine was flooded and sealed several decades ago, which means that Iraq would not have been able to obtain uranium there even if it tried.

Following the collapse of Saddam Hussein's government, the United States gained access to Iraqi government records and set up the Iraq Survey Group (ISG), a 1,200-person team that began combing through the country and interrogating former Iraqi officials in search of weapons of mass destruction. Its final report, published in September 2004, concluded that it could find no evidence of Iraq trying to procure uranium. The report added, moreover, that on the one known occasion when someone from another country approached Iraqi officials with an unsolicited offer to *sell* uranium, the Iraqis turned it down:

ISG has not found evidence to show that Iraq sought uranium from abroad after 1991 or renewed indigenous production of such material. . . . As part of its investigation, ISG sought information from prominent figures such as Jaífar Diyaí Jaífar—the head of the pre-1991 nuclear weapons program. . . .

Regarding specific allegations of uranium pursuits from Niger, Jaífar claims that after 1998 Iraq had only two contacts with [Niger's capital city of] Niamey—neither of which involved uranium. Jaífar acknowledged that Iraq's Ambassador to the Holy See traveled to Niamey to invite the President of Niger to visit Iraq. He indicated that Baghdad hoped that the Nigerian President would agree to the visit as he had visited Libya despite sanctions being levied on Tripoli. . . .

Jaífar claims a second contact between Iraq and Niger occurred when a Nigerian minister visited Baghdad around 2001 to request assistance in obtaining petroleum products to alleviate Niger's economic problems. During the negotiations for this contract, the Nigerians did not offer any kind of payment or other quid pro quo, including offering to provide Iraq with uranium ore, other than cash in exchange for petroleum.

ISG recovered a copy of a crude oil contract dated 26 June 2001 that, although unsigned, appears to support this arrangement.

So far, ISG has found only one offer of uranium to Baghdad since 1991—an approach Iraq appears to have turned down. In mid-May 2003, an ISG team found an Iraqi Embassy document in the Iraqi Intelligence Service (IIS) headquarters related to an offer to sell yellowcake to Iraq. The document reveals that a Ugandan businessman approached the Iraqis with an offer to sell uranium, reportedly from the Congo. The Iraqi Embassy in Nairobi—in reporting this matter back to Baghdad on 20 May 2001—indicated it told the Ugandan that Iraq does not deal with these materials, explained the circumstances of sanctions, and said that Baghdad was not concerned about these matters right now.[62]

In short, the evidence shows overwhelmingly that White House claims were false regarding Iraq's alleged efforts to purchase banned uranium ore. Administration officials had ample reason to know these claims were false at the time they were made, not just by President Bush but also by Paul Wolfowitz and Condoleezza Rice and Colin Powell. They certainly must have known that these claims were false by the time they set out to discredit Joseph Wilson and ruin the career of his wife. Finally, the evidence suggests that President Bush personally misled the public when he claimed in September 2003 not to know how his administration had leaked classified information.

In April 2006, defense filings by Libby indicated that Bush himself, as part of the effort to discredit Wilson, had authorized leaking its classified National Intelligence Estimate regarding the Niger-uranium issue.[63] Faced with this statement by the vice president's own former chief of staff, the White House did not attempt to deny it. Instead, press secretary Scott McClellan said the information had been leaked "in the public interest." Reporters asked how McClellan reconciled this claim with previous statements by himself and Bush, in which they had condemned leaks and denied knowing their source. McClellan replied that there was a "distinction" between leaking classified information versus "declassifying information and providing it to the public."[64] This was at best a fine distinction in service of a tortured argument, but without it, there was no choice but to admit that they had simply been lying.

CHAPTER THREE

Big Impact

Throughout the Joseph Wilson affair, the
White House argued that the yellowcake forgery was only a
small element in the portfolio of evidence it presented as its case
for war. Its claim about uranium from Niger, so it argued, was
only part of the evidence showing that Iraq had a covert nuclear
weapon program, which in turn was only part of the evidence
that Iraq already possessed an arsenal of banned chemical and
biological weapons—the "weapons of mass destruction" that
were the main reason for going to war. In Bush's 2003 State of
the Union speech before the war, he was quite specific. Iraq, he
said, possessed "over 25,000 liters of anthrax—enough doses to

kill several million people"; "more than 38,000 liters of botulinum toxin—enough to subject millions of people to death by respiratory failure"; "as much as 500 tons of sarin, mustard and VX nerve agent"; and "upwards of 30,000 munitions capable of delivering chemical agents."[1]

Eight days later, Colin Powell addressed the United Nations and laid out the charges in further detail. Powell said his evidence came from multiple, corroborating sources: Iraqi defectors, informants, intercepted radio messages, satellite photographs, and interrogation of detainees seized in Afghanistan and elsewhere since September 11. As he spoke, Powell displayed drawings, photographs, and audiotapes.[2] The speech, unusual in its detail and specificity, was almost universally praised the following day by U.S. newspapers and was seen by many as decisive in the public debate over whether to go to war. Gilbert Cranberg, the former editorial-page editor of the *Des Moines Register*, reviewed editorial comments in forty newspapers following the speech and found "unanimity as to Iraq's possession of weapons of mass destruction. . . . Journalists are supposed to be professional skeptics, but nowhere in the commentary was there a smidgen of skepticism about the quality of Powell's evidence."[3]

➤ A *New York Times* editorial called the speech a "sober, factual case," and a separate news article described it as "a nearly encyclopedic catalog that reached further than many had expected."[4] An analysis of the speech by *Times* reporter Michael Gordon stated that "it will be difficult for skeptics to argue that Washington's case against Iraq is based on groundless suspicions and not intelligence information."[5]

➤ Senator Joseph R. Biden, Jr., the senior Democrat on the Foreign Relations Committee, called Powell's speech "powerful and irrefutable." A *Washington Post* editorial agreed, adding that "it is hard to imagine how anyone could doubt that Iraq possesses weapons of mass destruction."[6]

➤ The *Los Angeles Times* editorialized that Powell had offered "solid evidence" and declared, "The United Nations risks irrelevance unless it promptly sets a date on which it will use military force against Iraq if that nation does not disarm."[7]

➤ "Mr. Powell eliminated any reasonable doubt," wrote the *Washington Times* in an editorial, adding, "In the wake of Mr. Powell's presentation, no reasonable person can doubt that Saddam is continuing his longstanding efforts to deceive the international community about his weapons programs."[8]

➤ "Only the blind could ignore Powell's evidence," wrote the *Dallas Morning News* editorial page, adding that Powell "did everything but perform cornea transplants on the countries that still claim to see no reason for forcibly disarming Iraq."[9]

➤ The *San Francisco Chronicle* called the speech "impressive in its breadth and eloquence."[10]

➤ The *Denver Post* said Powell had presented "not just one 'smoking gun' but a battery of them, more than sufficient to dispel any lingering doubt about the threat the Iraqi dictator poses."[11]

➤ California's *San Jose Mercury News* said Powell made his case "without resorting to exaggeration, a rhetorical tool he didn't need."[12]

What these editorials and analyses all had in common was their assumption that a major speech by the secretary of state could not possibly have been based on exaggeration or outright fabrications. As the *Washington Times* put it, the choice was to "concede" Powell's case "or be prepared to call Mr. Powell a liar."[13] No one was prepared to call Colin Powell a liar. Newspapers did not attempt to fact-check his presentation until months after it was delivered. The first notable critique appeared four months later, when *U.S. News & World Report* wrote about Powell's own incredulous reaction to the first draft of his speech— "I'm not reading this. This is bullshit!"[14] A couple of months later, Associated Press reporter Charles J. Hanley went through the speech, point by point, and wrote a devastating 2,500-word critique.[15] It would eventually become known that Powell's speech to the United Nations was riddled with statements that his own staff had flagged as "weak" and/or "not credible," but this fact did not emerge until later, after the United States had already gone to war, and the failure to find weapons in Iraq prompted congressional investigations and public scrutiny.[16]

White House claims about Iraq—and the failure of journalists to question those claims—were reflected in public opinion. Surveyed on July 2003, 70 percent of Americans said they believed Iraq had weapons of mass destruction before the war began. This belief died slowly. In January 2005, 54 percent *still* believed it—even though the Iraq Survey Group, the U.S. team charged with looking for WMDs, had by then completed its final report, in which it declared that it had found no evidence of weapons or even of significant weapons programs.[17]

"Know" Means "Know"

The Bush administration did not merely say it *suspected* that Iraq had weapons. It claimed to know for certain, and even to know where they were located. "We do know, with absolute certainty," said Dick Cheney, that Saddam Hussein "is using his procurement system to acquire the equipment he needs in order to enrich uranium to build a nuclear weapon."[18] In Colin Powell's speech to the United Nations, he said, "There can be *no doubt* that Saddam Hussein has biological weapons and the capability to rapidly produce more, many more."[19] President Bush made the same claim in his televised address to the nation announcing the start of war: "Intelligence gathered by this and other governments leaves no doubt that the Iraq regime continues to possess and conceal some of the most lethal weapons ever devised."[20]

The claim that Iraq possessed weapons of mass destruction was not just a component of the administration's case for war. It was its *main* argument. Three days before the commencement of fighting, Vice President Dick Cheney appeared on *Meet the Press* with Tim Russert and declared that "the front of our concerns as we try to deal with these issues is the proposition that

the al-Qaeda organization is absolutely determined to do everything they can to acquire chemical, biological, and nuclear
weapons. . . . But we also have to address the question of where
might these terrorists acquire weapons of mass destruction,
chemical weapons, biological weapons, nuclear weapons? And
Saddam Hussein becomes a prime suspect in that regard because of his past track record and because we know he has, in
fact, developed these kinds of capabilities, chemical and biological weapons. We know he's used chemical weapons. We
know he's reconstituted these programs since the Gulf War.
We know he's out trying once again to produce nuclear weapons
and we know that he has a long-standing relationship with various terrorist groups, including the al-Qaeda organization."

"What do you think is the most important rationale for going
to war with Iraq?" Russert asked.

"Well, I think I've just given it, Tim," Cheney replied, "in
terms of the combination of his development and use of chemical weapons, his development of biological weapons, his pursuit
of nuclear weapons."[21]

The belief that Iraq possessed banned weapons was not limited to the Bush administration. During the Iran-Iraq war of the
1980s, Iraq had actually used chemical weapons, and its nuclear
program had come closer to developing an actual bomb than
outside analysts realized at the time. Even among people who
opposed the U.S. war in 2003, it was widely suspected that Iraq
still possessed some of the banned weapons that it had developed prior to Operation Desert Storm in 1991. This assumption
was accepted by retired CIA analyst Ray McGovern, who
founded a group that opposed the war called Veteran Intelli-

gence Professionals for Sanity. McGovern accused the White House of using intelligence information that was "cooked to a recipe," and he did not believe that weapons existed in sufficient quantities to justify war. Even as he opposed the war, however, McGovern warned that the Bush administration was "sending U.S. forces into battle without adequate protection against Iraq's chemical and biological weapons. . . . Saddam, with his back to the wall, will unleash his arsenal of chemical and perhaps bio-logical weapons."[22]

Some opponents of the war, however, doubted that any weapons of significance remained at all. In the months before the war began, former United Nations weapons inspector Scott Ritter was adamant in stating that inspections had been able to "ascertain a 90 to 95 percent level of verified disarmament" and that any remaining chemical or biological agents produced prior to 1990 would have degraded within five years. The Bush administration's claims, he said, were "only speculation" lacking "any factually based information."[23]

The most notable—yet rarely noted—skepticism came from weapons inspectors with the United Nations Monitoring, Verifi-cation and Inspection Commission (UNMOVIC). Led by chief UN weapons inspector Hans Blix, they were the team actually engaged in on-the-ground inspections in Iraq during the months prior to the start of war. On the basis of U.S. intelligence tips and other information, the UNMOVIC inspectors had con-ducted hundreds of surprise visits to sites in Iraq, but none of them found banned weapons. According to one veteran inspec-tor, the intelligence tips that they received from the United States were "worthless to the point of embarrassment." After rushing out to investigate a chicken farm that turned out to contain nothing but chickens, one inspector had T-shirts made that lampooned their mission as "Ballistic Chicken Farm Inspectors."[24] A few days before the start of war, the UNMOVIC inspectors were pulled out of the country, expressing anger as they left at the Bush administration for forcing them to cut short their work. According to one inspector, Iraq was "a ruined country, not a threat to anyone." Another said the country's weapons infrastructure was so decrepit that at most, its covert weapons program might consist of "a few guys with paper and pencil and some computer in a back room."[25] In an interview recorded hours before the first missiles struck Baghdad, Hans Blix expressed doubt that Iraq possessed weapons of mass destruction and said he was "curious" to learn what Americans would find when they occupied the country.[26]

The White House, however, harbored no such doubts. Two weeks into the war, the United States had already taken control of ten sites deemed to be of "urgent" interest because they were believed to contain chemical warheads, Scud missiles, and missile launchers. Nothing found at any of those sites suggested WMDs, but Donald Rumsfeld shrugged off the findings, claiming that the banned weapons were in areas not yet controlled by U.S.-led forces. "We know where they are," he said. "They are in the area around Tikrit and Baghdad and east, west, south, and north of that."[27]

The Fog Machine of War

For many people, including journalists who traveled embedded with U.S. troops in Iraq, the Bush administration's confident affirmations of certainty seemed to have an almost hypnotic effect. Soldiers and their accompanying reporters kept seeking—and in many cases, finding—mysterious hints, suspicious items, and tantalizing clues that seemed to be the "smoking gun" that would prove once and for all that Iraq harbored banned weapons. The discoveries were treated on page one in major newspapers and as breaking news on television. Later, when it came time to admit that these discoveries were mistaken, the retractions were buried on inside pages or omitted altogether.

➤ On March 28, 2003, NBC correspondent David Bloom reported "a bit of a chemical weapons scare" when "U.S. military intelligence picked up what they suspected to be three possibly mobile chemical/biological trucks."[28] The tanker trucks were bombed by U.S. aircraft and spent the rest of the day burning, suggesting that they probably contained fuel rather than chemical or biological agents.[29]

➤ That same day, the *New York Times* cited intelligence reports from army officials that Saddam Hussein was setting up a ring of chemical weapons—a "red line" defense—to surround Baghdad, and "strongly believed that Mr. Hussein would use the weapons as allied troops moved toward

Baghdad to oust him and his government."[30] This also turned out to be a mirage.[31]

➤ On April 4, U.S. troops took possession of the Latifiyah Explosives and Ammunition Plant south of Baghdad and reported that they had found boxes of white powder that a commander called "suspicious."[32] MSNBC'S Chris Matthews asked analyst David Kay about the powder. "Chris, get ready," Kay said. "We're going to have a lot more of these. We're now driving into the heartland of Iraq's WMD program, the area where he produced and stored it. It's the area around Baghdad and Tikrit."[33] The white powder was tested and found to be conventional explosives— the sort of thing you might *expect* to find at an explosives plant.[34]

➤ On April 7, National Public Radio's John Burnett reported that "a top military official here with the 1st Marine Division" had found "the first solid confirmed existence of chemical weapons by the Iraqi army. He says a relatively large amount, perhaps 20 medium-range rockets, were found with warheads containing sarin, a nerve gas, and mustard gas, which is a blister agent. They had not been fired. They were captured. . . . If it turns out to be true, the commander told us this morning this would be a smoking gun. This would vindicate the administration's claims that the Iraqis had chemicals all along." The NPR report was picked up and repeated by other media. Later that day, the Pentagon backed off the story. "That report has not been confirmed by the Pentagon," reported NPR's Jennifer Ludden. "However, U.S. officials have cited the discovery of suspicious chemicals apparently in 50-gallon drums that are in a warehouse along the Euphrates River southwest of Baghdad." NPR never followed up on the story, leaving listeners to guess or surmise the contents of the 50-gallon drums.[35]

➤ On MSNBC that same day, Dana Lewis reported the discovery in Karbala of "chemical barrels in an agricultural factory. . . . What they have found is eleven twenty-five-gallon barrels and three fifty-five-gallon barrels. They were buried very suspiciously in a bunker. . . . They have run tests on this. And what they have found is sarin and tabun, which are nerve agents. And we are also told that they have found a mustard-type agent."[36] News reports also noted that several soldiers in the vicinity had collapsed, adding to suspicions that they had been exposed to a chemical agent. The *Miami Herald* carried a headline declaring "Discovery at Village the Strongest Signs of Toxins Yet." Further tests showed that the barrels contained farm pesticides. Troops also found pamphlets describing how to deal with mosquitoes, and it turned out that the soldiers who collapsed had suffered heat stroke.[37] A few British newspapers carried the correction that WMDs had not been found after all, but the correction was omitted altogether or buried near the bottom of stories in U.S. newspapers, which by then were agog with other new and alarming discoveries—discoveries that also led nowhere in the end.

Fox Trots

The Fox News network had the dubious honor of reporting more WMD discoveries than any other network. Its sensational reports from Iraq were so popular with conservative viewers that it won the cable ratings war during the invasion of Iraq, even though Fox had a smaller contingent of correspondents actually reporting from the battlefield than any of the others. At the time of the Iraq war, Fox News had just 1,250 full-time and freelance employees and seventeen news bureaus, only six of them overseas, with operating costs of about $250 million. By contrast, CNN had four thousand employees and forty-two bureaus, thirty-one of them overseas, at a cost of about $800 million. In the Middle East, Fox had only fifteen correspondents, compared to at least one hundred apiece for ABC, CBS, NBC, and BBC.[38] As U.S. tanks rolled on Baghdad, Fox was forced to purchase video footage of Baghdad from Al Jazeera, the Arab network.

"We don't have the resources overseas that CNN and other networks have," admitted Fox correspondent Rick Leventhal, who was with the First Marine Light Armor Reconnaissance unit. "We're going in with less money and equipment and people, and trying to do the same job. You might call it smoke and mirrors, but it's working."[39] The "smoke and mirrors" consisted of opinionated pundits and studio consultants, who filled the gaps left by their limited reporting from the field with a free-wheeling mix of wild speculation, embellishments of reports from other journalists, and outright fantasy. Here are some of the reports that viewers saw on Fox News during just one ten-minute time slice on April 9. Note the absence of references to specific, verifiable individuals or locations:

➤ *1:00 p.m.:* "Possible weapons of mass destruction storage site also detected in central Baghdad."

➤ *1:04 p.m.:* "Fox News alert for you from the front, of course, they have found what they have suspected was a chemical facility that might have been weapons. Well, they've done initial tests on those big drums, those many-gallon container drums they have, and apparently according to initial tests, banned chemical weapons have been found in Iraq. This is hot off the wire, it is breaking information; this could be the so-called smoking gun. . . . Apparently some military folks went in there, discovered these drums, got sick, they started to vomit, there were skin rashes."

➤ *1:08 p.m.:* "Nerve agents . . . have been found, also a blister agent; now this was in a part of Iraq that is in the centrally located area where U.S. marines had gone in, found these big containers, these huge vats, gallons of stuff that made the folks in there sick. . . . Remnants of sarin, tabun, and a blister agent . . . have been found in Iraq."[40]

On March 23, the Associated Press reported that troops had found a "suspected chemical plant" near the city of Najaf, noting that the discovery had not been confirmed.[41] Fox News announced the story by running headline banners that said,

"HUGE CHEMICAL WEAPONS FACTORY FOUND IN SO IRAQ. . . . REPORTS: 30 IRAQIS SURRENDER AT CHEM WEAPONS PLANT. . . . COAL TROOPS HOLDING IRAQI IN CHARGE OF CHEM WEAPONS." The story on their website said the discovery had been confirmed by "a senior Pentagon official."[42] Fox anchor Linda Vester told viewers, "This validates President Bush's argument with the UN. . . . This is proof that Saddam has been hiding weapons of mass destruction." The following morning, Pentagon officials backed away from the story. No chemicals had been found there at all, in what appeared upon examination to be a long-abandoned facility.

On April 10, an embedded reporter from the *Pittsburgh Tribune-Review* wrote that "a quick inspection" by army specialists at the Tuwaitha Nuclear Research Center had sparked suspicions that the site "harbors weapons-grade plutonium."[43] Prior to 1991, the Tuwaitha facility had been part of Iraq's nuclear weapons program, but it was bombed by the United States during Operation Desert Storm and subsequently monitored and regulated by the IAEA. Fox News recycled the *Pittsburgh Tribune-Review* story into a "breaking news" special, featuring interviews with stateside military analysts and a scientist who said, "I think this demonstrates the failure of the UN weapons inspections and demonstrates that our guys are going to find the weapons of mass destruction."[44] Neither Fox nor the *Pittsburgh Tribune-Review* mentioned that the Tuwaitha facility had actually been subject to continuous on-site UN monitoring for years. And Fox did not bother correcting the record when, days later, further investigations found no evidence of plutonium or other banned nuclear weapons components.

Also on April 10, Fox reported the discovery of a small, shot-up, tan-colored truck that they described as "a mobile unit, disguised as . . . a surface-to-air missile radar truck. . . . Upon closer inspection, they discovered a false wall. What was behind that false wall? Well, all sorts of material that would suggest this was, in fact, a chemical-biological weapons mobile lab. Winches to lift things up, areas to cool and to warm certain things. Bottles, test tubes. Other materials suggestive of the presence at some point in the past of weapons that could have been used in a chemical or biological attack. . . . This could be the first explicit piece of evidence that a mobile-chemical-biological weapons truck existed. And it was right in the heart of Baghdad. And as Rick Leventhal reported, at least when it was discovered, less than half a block from the UN offices where weapons inspectors had once worked."[45] The following day, Fox interviewed G. Gordon Liddy, who boasted that the "biolab special truck was discovered by my son, Major Ray Liddy in the Marine Corps, his unit, 23rd Marines, 2nd Battalion. . . . But guess who that specialized truck was traced to, who manufactured it for them? The French." After some general ridicule of France, Democrats, and peaceniks in San Francisco, Fox cohost Alan Colmes was allowed to counter, "I think they've decided it is not a weapons of mass destruction mobile lab."[46] Nothing further has ever been heard about the little tan truck.

On May 8, another Fox analyst, retired general Paul Vallely, told Bill O'Reilly he had evidence that the WMDs had been smuggled into Syria and were buried thirty to forty meters underground in the Bekaa Valley. He added that the government of France had provided forged passports to help Saddam flee the country. "Let me stop you," O'Reilly interrupted. "Do you really believe there's going to be conclusive proof, General, do you believe there is going to be conclusive proof that France helped Saddam Hussein and his thugs escape? Do you believe that will come out?"

"Absolutely," Vallely replied. "There is enough information, Bill, that I'm getting coming out that is going to bury and break the Chirac government."

"Wow!" said O'Reilly.[47]

Eight months later, Saddam Hussein was captured inside Iraq in an underground "spider hole" near his hometown of Tikrit. Evidently his wine-swilling, Brie-eating French accomplices were so fearful upon being exposed by the intrepid journalists at Fox that they smuggled the tyrant back into Iraq to face his fate.

WMD or Not to Be

Shortly after the fall of Baghdad, a survey conducted by the University of Maryland found that 34 percent of Americans believed that weapons of mass destruction had actually been found in Iraq, and 22 percent believed that WMDs had actually been *used* during the war. Sixty percent, moreover, believed that evidence of Iraq having WMDs was the most important reason to go to war. "Given the intensive news coverage and high levels of public attention to the topic, this level of misinformation suggests that some Americans may be avoiding having an experience of cognitive dissonance," suggested survey director Steven Kull.[48] Given the type of reporting we have described above, however, another likely possibility is that Americans got their misinformation *from* the news coverage they witnessed.

Given the extraordinary importance placed on WMDs as a rationale for war, the belief in their existence could not be abandoned easily or quickly. In the absence of actual weapons, the website of the U.S. Department of Defense posted photographs of chemical suits, Geiger counters, and gas masks found in Iraq—evidence, they said, that the regime must have weapons as well. As it became increasingly clear that actual weapons were not going to be found, administration officials adopted strategies aimed at buying time while they recalibrated their rhetoric to lower the expectations that they had previously raised.

Baghdad fell to U.S.-led forces on April 9, 2003. The following day, Kenneth Adelman, a member of the U.S. Defense Policy Board and a leading Iraq war hawk, predicted that "people will step forward pretty fast" to identify weapons stores. "It should be pretty soon, in the next five days," he said.[49]

"Make no mistake," said White House spokesman Ari Fleischer at a press briefing on April 10. "We have high confidence that they have weapons of mass destruction. That is what this war was about and is about. And we have high confidence it will be found."[50]

However, the U.S. refused to allow United Nations weapons inspectors back into the country to resume their work. "The president is looking forward, not backward," Fleischer said. "The Iraqi regime that created the environment for the inspectors previously to go in no longer exists. . . . The United States and the coalition have taken on the responsibility for dismantling Iraq's WMD."[51]

The refusal angered Hans Blix, who began to say openly that he thought Iraq probably had no WMDs after all. In an interview with BBC, he recalled that the tips he received from British and U.S. intelligence had not panned out when investigated on the ground. "Only in three of those cases did we find anything at all, and in none of these cases were there any weapons of mass destruction, and that shook me a bit, I must say," Blix said, adding, "I thought—my God, if this is the best intelligence they have and we find nothing, what about the rest?"[52]

For weapons to exist, of course, *someone* has to know where they are located. Upon capturing Baghdad, the United States took Iraq's top government officials into custody for interrogation. It compiled a list of three thousand priority locations in Iraq to search, including ninety locations that were considered the top sites most likely to contain banned weapons. The team assigned to search for weapons was called the 75th Exploitation Task Force. Staffed with biologists, chemists, arms treaty enforcers, nuclear operators, computer and document experts, and special forces troops, it fanned out to search the sites. Initially the team was full of high hopes and expectations as it searched laboratories, munitions plants, distilleries, bakeries and even holes in the ground where they received tips telling them to dig. Within a month, however, enthusiasm turned to sarcasm as they visited site after site with no results.[53]

Washington Post reporter Barton Gellman accompanied some of the weapons hunters and witnessed their findings. At site 26, they found a cache of vacuum cleaners, air conditioners, and rolls of fabric; at another, a distillery; at another, a swimming pool; a middle school for girls; a factory that manufactured license plates. Sometimes the weapons teams found suspicious-looking items, but upon examination the discoveries turned out to be innocuous. After some initial excitement about a document that included sketches of laboratory flasks, the soldiers realized that all they had uncovered was "some kid's high school science project," Gellman reported. And so it went: "Another day brought 'suspicious glass globes,' filled, as it turned out, with cleaning fluid. A drum of foul-smelling liquid revealed itself as used motor oil."[54]

The last notable claim that WMDs had actually been found came in May, after troops found a couple of mobile trailers in northern Iraq whose design loosely resembled the design for mobile bioweapons laboratories that Colin Powell had displayed during his speech to the United Nations. Following the usual script for such discoveries, NBC News correspondent Jim Avila reported from Baghdad that the trailers "may be the most significant WMD findings of the war." The CIA rushed out an analysis claiming that the trailers found in Iraq were indeed biowarfare labs. "We'll find more weapons as time goes on," Bush said on May 30. "But for those who say we haven't found the banned manufacturing devices or banned weapons, they're wrong. We found them."[55]

After examining the trailers, however, a team of engineering experts from the U.S. Defense Intelligence Agency disagreed, as did a report published two weeks later by British analysts. "They are not mobile germ warfare laboratories," said a British scientist. "You could not use them for making biological weapons. They do not even look like them. They are exactly what the Iraqis said they were—facilities for the production of hydrogen gas to fill balloons."[56] The Bush administration continued to insist that the trailers were bioweapons labs for months in the face of accumulating evidence to the contrary. By July 2003, however, their own chief weapons inspector on the ground in Iraq had backed away from the story, calling it a "fiasco."[57]

On June 1, 2003, senators from both the Republican and Democratic parties announced plans to hold hearings aimed at evaluating intelligence information about weapons of mass destruction. If WMDs are not found, said Florida senator Bob Graham, it would indicate either "a very serious intelligence failure, or the attempt to keep the American people in the dark by manipulating that intelligence information." Senate Armed Services Committee chairman John Warner was less critical but agreed that hearings should be held. "My credibility is on the line, because I relied on that same intelligence," Warner said.[58]

Shut Up and Wait

In August 2003, the Pentagon adopted a new strategy, called the "big impact" plan. According to *Washington Times* columnists Bill Gertz and Rowan Scarborough, "The plan calls for gathering and holding on to all the information now being collected about the weapons. Rather than releasing its findings piecemeal, defense officials will release a comprehensive report on the arms, perhaps six months from now. The goal of the strategy will be to quiet critics of the Bush administration who said claims of Iraq's hidden weapons stockpiles were exaggerated in order to go to war."[59]

At a news conference, Bush said, "It's going to take time for us to gather the evidence and analyze the mounds of evidence, literally, the miles of documents that we have uncovered. . . . And it's just going to take a while, and I'm confident the truth will come out." At the same time, a subtle but telling change entered his rhetoric. Whereas previously he had talked about actual *weapons*, instead he began talking about a weapons *program*. "I'm confident," he said, "that our search will yield that which I strongly believe, that Saddam had a weapons program."[60]

David Kay, a former UN inspector and supporter of the war with Iraq, was appointed as a special adviser to the Iraq Survey Group (ISG), the U.S. team assigned to replace the 75th Exploitation Task Force in the hunt for WMDs. To find the weapons, the ISG had a staff of 1,200 people and a budget of $300 million. On *NewsHour with Jim Lehrer*, Condoleezza Rice explained the plan: "What the president said to David Kay is, take your time; do this in a comprehensive way; do this in a way that makes the case, that looks at all of the evidence, and then tells us the truth about this program. What David Kay did say to me and to others is that this is a program that was built for deception over many, many years. . . . And so it's not surprising that it's going to take some time to really put this picture together. David Kay is going to put this together in a way that is coherent. I think that there is a danger in taking a little piece of evidence here, a little piece of evidence there. He is a very respected and capable weapons inspector. He knows how to read the Iraqi programs. . . . We will put this case together."[61]

At a news conference following a closed hearing with the Senate Intelligence Committee, Kay combined inscrutability with a tantalizing hint that "big impact" would be really, really big: "The American people should not be surprised by surprises," he said, adding that his team was finding new evidence of how Iraq "successfully misled inspections of the UN and hid stuff continuously from them. The active deception program is truly amazing once you get inside it."[62]

Kay was vague, however, when asked whether actual weapons had been found. "I think we are making solid progress," he said. "It is, as with most progress, it is preliminary. We are not at the final stage of understanding fully Iraq's WMD program or having found WMD weapons. It's going to take time. . . . I think the basis for that progress is solid in terms of the people and capabilities we have there. . . . My experience is when you get good people together with good equipment and they're well led that they usually outperform your expectations of how they move. I think it's very likely that we will discover remarkable surprises in this enterprise." Pressed further, he said, "I'm not going to talk to you about detailed evidence at this stage. That's not the way we're going to conduct this operation."[63]

After all the hemming and hawing, "big impact" was just another catchphrase. Like "shock and awe," it sounded impressive, but it was simply an effort to buy time and deflect attention away from the failure to actually find the weapons. The White House said it would take at least six months before the public should expect to see Kay's report. During that period, the Bush team could hope that public attention would wander elsewhere, while they adjusted their rhetoric to lower expectations about whatever they eventually offered as "proof."

Almost immediately after Kay arrived in Iraq, he realized that what he was looking for wasn't there. "Every weekend I wrote a private e-mail to the [director of Central Intelligence] and the [deputy director of Central Intelligence], my unvarnished summary of where we were," Kay later told a reporter. "I wrote that it looks as though they did not produce weapons." At best, he told them, Saddam's policy may have been "to produce actual weapons only close to the time you actually need them."[64]

The Hunt for the Real Duper

A month later, U.S. intelligence officials floated a new theory. Saddam Hussein had deceived people, all right—not by *hiding* weapons, but by acting suspicious so everyone would *believe they existed*. Bob Drogin, a reporter for the *Los Angeles Times*, interviewed an anonymous "senior U.S. intelligence official" who said intelligence agencies suspected that Saddam had tricked them using double agents disguised as Iraqi defectors who were sent out to spread disinformation. The agencies were reviewing their information, he said, "to see if false information was put out there and got into legitimate channels and we were totally duped on it." This, of course, would mean that Saddam Hussein actually suckered the United States into overthrowing his government, killing his sons, and putting him on trial—not exactly the sharpest scheme ever concocted. Officials floated a variety of possible motives to explain why Hussein might have done this: Maybe he was trying to look stronger militarily than he really was. Maybe he had some complicated scheme to embarrass the weapons inspectors and get sanctions lifted. "We're looking at that and every other possibility," the intelligence official said. "You can't rule anything out. . . . People are really second-guessing themselves now."[65]

"We were prisoners of our own beliefs," said another senior U.S. weapons expert. "We said Saddam Hussein was a master of denial and deception. Then when we couldn't find anything, we said that proved it, instead of questioning our own assumptions."[66]

On September 7, 2003, the White House announced that David Kay was about to present a preliminary report to Congress on the findings of the Iraq Survey Group. "I am confident when people see what David Kay puts forward they will see that there was no question that such weapons exist, existed, and so did the programs to develop one," said Colin Powell. "We did not try to hype it or blow it out of proportion."[67]

A week later, however, word leaked out that the progress report, expected on September 15, had been delayed and that Kay was finding so little of substance that a final report might never be published. Public officials were vague when asked about his progress. Donald Rumsfeld acknowledged that he had met with Kay earlier that month but said he hadn't asked whether Kay had found any WMDs. On September 22, Condoleezza Rice said there "may" be interim reports from the Iraq Survey Group, but "I don't know what the public nature of them will be." CIA spokesman Bill Harlow said, "Don't expect any firm conclusions."[68]

Even Fox News correspondent Mansoor Ijaz began preparing rationales for the eventuality that weapons would not be found. Maybe, he argued, the weapons had been buried somewhere in the desert where no one could find them. "Let us assume for the sake of argument that Saddam or his two sons gave the order to bury the stuff that they had just before the war started in the sand somewhere in the Iraqi desert. If they did—and conceivably the people who did it were then either assassinated by Saddam himself or killed in the war. We now know that two of those three people are dead. The sons are now dead. So therefore, the people who had the knowledge of exactly where this stuff would be, in a country that's the size of California—they may no longer have the capacity to give us the information because they're not alive anymore."[69]

On October 2, Kay finally delivered the interim report and tried to put the best face on things. "We have not yet found stocks of weapons, but we are not yet at the point where we can say definitively either that such weapon stocks do not exist," he said. Kay added hopefully that his team was still hard at work and that they had found "dozens of WMD-related program activities and significant amounts of equipment that Iraq concealed from the United Nations during the inspections that began in late 2002."[70] But when a reporter asked if he had found any weapons of mass destruction, Kay replied, "I've barely found lunch."[71]

The White House continued to fuzz up its rhetoric. Previously it had gone from declaring that Iraq had weapons to talking about weapons *programs*. Now it was reduced to talking of "program *activities*" and evidence of mere *intent* to relaunch weapons programs at some unspecified moment in the future. But was something as vague as a dictator's future dreams sufficient cause to justify a war? In an interview on ABC News, Diane Sawyer asked Bush to comment on the difference between claiming that Saddam Hussein actually *had* "weapons of mass destruction, as opposed to the possibility that he could move to acquire those weapons."

"What's the difference?" Bush replied. "The possibility that he could acquire weapons, if he were to acquire weapons, he would be the danger."[72] In his State of the Union address the following month, Bush said that Kay's group had found evidence of "WMD-related program activities" in Iraq but avoided any mention of the broader point that no actual weapons had been found. The revised standard that Bush now offered as his rationale for war was the mere *possibility* of acquiring weapons in the future. By that standard, though, Iraq had actually presented less of a threat than Pakistan, which was officially considered an ally in the war on terror even as it was caught providing the technology for nuclear weapons to Iran, Libya, and North Korea.[73]

Reality Bites

On January 7, 2004, the *Washington Post* published a page-one story by Barton Gellman. The title said it all: "Iraq's Arsenal Was Only on Paper." The Iraq Survey Group's search had not been completely fruitless, but it came close. After combing through Iraq for months and spending $300 million, the inspectors did find some attempts by Iraq to violate prohibitions on its weapons development. The activities that they found, however, were largely in research and development, most of which had made little progress. An Iraqi rocket scientist, for example, had developed preliminary plans for longer-range missiles than the country was allowed to produce. But turning those plans into actual missiles would have taken years—if they ever worked at all.[74] The Iraq Survey Group also found some items that were evidence of deception in the early 1990s, most notably a centrifuge buried in a rose garden. The centrifuge, which had been developed as part of Iraq's effort prior to 1991 to refine uranium for a nuclear bomb, had been buried ever since in the backyard of Dr. Mahdi Obeidi, a nuclear scientist who worked on the program. Obeidi said he had buried the centrifuge and blueprints on orders from Saddam Hussein's son Qusay, but he had heard nothing further from the regime about it since 1992. Another scientist showed them a vial of botulinum bacteria that he had kept in his refrigerator at home since 1993. Like Obeidi's centrifuge, it was a relic of Iraq's abandoned weapons programs. For ten years, nobody in the Iraqi government had shown the slightest interest in reclaiming it or using it, not even after United Nations weapons inspectors left the country in 1998.

The Iraq Survey Group also found information that undercut expectations of any further weapons discoveries. During the buildup to war, administration officials had repeatedly cited information gleaned about Iraq's weapons programs from Hussein Kamel, Saddam's son-in-law, who defected to Jordan in 1995. At the time of his defection, Kamel was debriefed by United Nations weapons inspectors and gave them information about Iraq's concealed weapons programs—revelations that angered Saddam Hussein so much that Kamel was lured back to Iraq and killed. White House officials had cited Kamel's revelations as evidence that Iraq had not disarmed and that inspections were not working. What they failed to mention, however, was that Kamel had also told interrogators that Iraq's actual *weapons* were all destroyed shortly after the end of the first Gulf War. All that remained, Kamel said, were "hidden blueprints, computer disks, microfiches," and production molds.[75]

Of course, defectors from Iraq cannot be counted on to be 100 percent truthful, and it was possible to imagine that Hussein Kamel had withheld information from his interrogators. The Iraq Survey Group's investigations, however, uncovered an internal memorandum from Saddam Hussein's presidential office in response to Kamel's defection. Written for the purposes of damage control, the memo described the regime's secrets that Kamel had carried with him. Kamel's debriefings and subsequent inspections by the United Nations Special Commission (UNSCOM) had exposed every item on the list. The memo confirmed, in short, that Iraq had—reluctantly, to be sure—destroyed its entire inventory of banned weapons.[76]

Realizing that the search was fruitless, David Kay had tried to resign from the Iraq Survey Group in December 2003, but delayed his announcement at the request of CIA director George Tenet, who told him, "If you resign now it will appear like we don't know what we're doing and the wheels are coming off."[77] He waited to resign publicly until January 23—three days after Bush's State of the Union address. A few days later, he testified before the U.S. Senate about his findings. "Let me begin by saying we were almost all wrong, and I certainly include myself here," he said.

Senator John Warner responded by pointing out that Iraq was a country the size of California and wondering if Kay's conclusion was premature. Maybe if they looked longer, Warner suggested, they would find something.

That was possible in theory, Kay replied, but highly unlikely. In addition to looking for weapons, the Iraq Survey Group had also looked for evidence of production processes. "When you don't find them in the obvious places, you look to see: Were they produced? Were there people that produced them? Were there the inputs to the production process? And you do that and you eliminate." Based on those inquiries, he said, "I believe that the effort that has been directed to this point has been sufficiently intense that it is highly unlikely that there were large stockpiles of deployed militarized chemical and biological weapons there."

Senator John McCain asked another question: "Obviously, we were wrong, as you said. Now, *why* were we wrong?"

"Senator, I wouldn't pretend that I know all the answers or even know all the questions to get at that," Kay replied.[78]

Following Kay's resignation, Charles Duelfer was appointed to complete the work of the Iraq Survey Group. Its final report, published on September 30, 2004, devoted most of its pages to damning assessments of Saddam Hussein's personality, the brutal nature of his dictatorship, and his history of past deceptions and weapons-related activities. It spoke of Iraq's "byzantine setting," "culture of lies," "command by violence," "mutuality of fear," "Saddam's psychology," and "veiled WMD intent." In the end, though, the report admitted, "ISG has not found evidence that Saddam Husayn possessed WMD stocks in 2003." At most, the report left open "the possibility that some weapons existed in Iraq although not of a militarily significant capability."[79]

Whereas once the United States had sought weapons, now the government turned to seeking the source of the illusion that weapons ever existed. Here, too, the searchers seemed unable to find what they were looking for. President Bush appointed a Commission on the Intelligence Capabilities of the United States Regarding Weapons of Mass Destruction. After a year of poring through evidence and interviewing experts, the commission issued a 601-page report (known as the Silberman-Robb report, after its lead authors), which reached the following conclusion:

> The harm done to American credibility by our all too public intelligence failings in Iraq will take years to undo. If there is good news it is this: without actually suffering a massive nuclear or biological attack, we have learned how badly the Intelligence Community can fail in struggling to understand the most important threats we face. . . .
>
> As war loomed, the U.S. Intelligence Community was charged with telling policymakers what it knew about Iraq's nuclear, biological, and chemical weapons programs. The Community's best assessments were . . . that Iraq was still pursuing its programs for weapons of mass destruction (WMD). Specifically, the [National Intelligence Estimate] assessed that Iraq had reconstituted its nuclear weapons program and could assemble a device by the end of the decade; that Iraq had biological weapons and mobile facilities for producing biological warfare (BW) agent; that Iraq had both renewed production of chemical weapons, and probably had chemical weapons stockpiles of up to 500 metric tons; and that Iraq was developing unmanned aerial vehicles (UAVs) probably intended to deliver BW agent.
>
> These assessments were all wrong.[80]

To prevent similar failings in the future, the commission called for "forging an integrated intelligence community," restructuring the management of U.S. intelligence operations, and having the White House "improve its mechanisms for watching over the intelligence community."[81] However, the commission made no effort to even ask whether existing White House "mechanisms for watching over the intelligence community" might have actually been part of the problem. Its recommendations for administrative reform were so general, impersonal, and structural in nature that no individuals could be held to account. No one lost their job. No one was indicted, accused, reprimanded, or disciplined. CIA director George Tenet had overseen U.S. intelligence reports on Iraq that the commission now called "a major intelligence failure" of a magnitude that "we simply cannot afford."[82] Rather than disgrace, he received the Presidential Medal of Honor from President Bush.

CHAPTER FOUR

Our Man in Baghdad

AT THE END OF WORLD WAR I, THE AUSTRIAN
journalist Karl Wiegand made an interesting observation. "How
are nations ruled and led into war?" he asked. "Politicians lie to
journalists and then believe those lies when they see them in
print." This may seem cynical, but it is a remarkably apt description of the process by which the United States ended up invading Iraq.

The war with Iraq, however, introduced one innovation that
Wiegand did not contemplate. In this instance, U.S. politicians
actually created a third party to do the lying for them—
specifically, Ahmed Chalabi and his Iraqi National Congress

(INC). "With Chalabi, we paid to fool ourselves," said former CIA counterterrorism expert Vincent Cannistraro. "It's horrible. In other times, it might be funny. But a lot of people are dead as a result of this. It's reprehensible."[1]

When we wrote *Weapons of Mass Deception* in 2003, we provided a summary of what was known at the time about Chalabi and the INC—a front group that was originally created in the early 1990s by a public relations firm, acting on orders from President George Herbert Walker Bush. Much of the details of its activities were still unknown to the public at that time, but subsequent government inquiries and journalistic investigations have provided a wealth of new information that expands our picture of the INC and the crucial role it played as a shaper of perceptions in the United States. From the outset, the INC's mission was to create conditions that would lead to the toppling of Saddam Hussein's regime in Iraq, and of course that is exactly what it accomplished. In an expansive moment, INC aide Francis Brooke boasted to *New Yorker* staff writer Jane Mayer about the "amazing success" of his public relations strategy. "This war would not have been fought if it had not been for Ahmed," Brooke said.[2]

In order to achieve this objective, however, the Iraqi National Congress spun a web of disinformation that seems to have successfully deceived even its sponsors in the U.S. government. Using funding provided by the United States, the INC managed to position itself as a central source for much of the now-discredited "intelligence information" that was used publicly to justify the March 2003 invasion. Six months later, an internal assessment conducted by the U.S. Defense Intelligence Agency concluded that most of the information provided by INC-supplied defectors—for which the U.S. paid millions of dollars—was worthless.[3] By then, however, the damage was done.

The INC's activities also appear to violate the terms of its funding agreement with the United States. The INC was supposed to "implement a public information campaign to communicate with Iraqis inside and outside of Iraq and also to promulgate its message to the international community at large." However, the agreement also stipulated that the INC's activities should "strictly exclude" activities "associated with, or that could appear to be associated with, attempting to influence the policies of the United States Government or Congress, or propagandizing the American people."[4] In fact, the INC's most significant accomplishment was its success at influencing U.S. policies and propagandizing the American public.

Creation of a Front Group

The INC got its start in the aftermath of Operation Desert Storm. With Saddam Hussein still in control of Iraq, President George Herbert Walker Bush authorized a covert CIA operation to "create the conditions for removal of Saddam Hussein from power." The agency—unequipped to execute the president's "lethal finding" itself but with access to ready money—outsourced the job to the Rendon Group, a shadowy public relations firm, based in

Washington, D.C., that specializes in behind-the-scenes assistance to U.S. military operations overseas.

There were at least two arms to Rendon's INC operation: a London-based media campaign that publicized the Iraqi dictator's human-rights abuses, and a behind-the-scenes effort to create an opposition group within Iraq that would, in the words of *Time* magazine, "gather information, distribute propaganda, and recruit dissidents."[5] Working with the CIA, the Rendon Group created an umbrella organization for Iraqi dissidents, naming it the Iraqi National Congress. The polished and charming international financer Ahmed Chalabi, even though he had recently been convicted of bank fraud in Jordan, was a CIA favorite and assumed a starring role in the organization.

According to a February 1998 ABC News report, the Rendon Group funneled $12 million in covert CIA funding to the INC between 1992 and 1996.[6] Reportedly, Rendon's secret contract with the CIA guaranteed the firm a 10 percent "management fee" in addition to operation expenses. The INC's London office offered stories of Saddam's atrocities to British journalists, many of which got picked up by the U.S. press. In northern Iraq, Rendon set up two anti-Hussein broadcasting operations and provided them with media training and propaganda. Robert Baer, a former CIA officer who covered Iraq, told the *New Yorker*'s Jane Mayer that Chalabi had a "forgery shop" set up in Kurdistan. But as far as being a viable opposition to Saddam, the INC's operation was "just a Potemkin village," Baer said. Chalabi "was reporting no intel; it was total trash. The INC's intelligence was so bad, we weren't even sending it in."[7] When the operation fell apart, a deep rift developed between the INC and CIA. While each blamed the other for being ineffective, the operation's failure did not receive much public or congressional attention. Unchecked, many of the key players stayed in the game.

Mr. Chalabi Goes to Washington

For the next two years, Chalabi lived in Washington, making new friends and securing financing for the group. He was joined by Francis Brooke, an American whose pre-Rendon experience including lobbying for the beer industry. The two shared a Georgetown row house owned by Chalabi's family and began to cultivate Republican congressmen. Chalabi impressed conservatives like Dick Cheney, Newt Gingrich, Trent Lott, Richard Perle, and Paul Wolfowitz, befriending them and gaining support for his plan to achieve a Saddam-free Iraq. "We thought very carefully about this, and realized there were only a couple of hundred people" in Washington who were influential in shaping policy toward Iraq," Brooke said.[8]

The lobbying paid off with the passage of the Iraq Liberation Act of 1998, which promised $97 million in aid to the INC and other opposition groups for "establishing a program [to] support a transition to democracy in Iraq." Part of this money was spent to support more lobbying in Washington. Between 1999 and 2003, the INC retained BKSH & Associates, the Washington lobbying arm of public relations giant Burson-Marsteller. K. Riva Levinson, a managing director at BKSH, did media work and lobbying for the group. According to Brooke, BKSH received $25,000 a month from the INC, notwithstanding restrictions on taxpayer money being spent to influence public and congressional opinion.

Within the public relations industry, the money was seen as well spent. *PR Week*, an industry trade publication, gave Burson-Marsteller and the INC its 2003 public affairs division award for building the INC's "profile with key political decision makers in the US, Europe and the Middle East. Of particular importance was positioning INC founder Dr. Ahmad Chalabi and other Iraqi opposition spokespeople as authoritative political leaders. With teams working in Washington, New York, London and Europe, B-M compiled intelligence reports, defector briefings, conferences and seminars on the transition of Iraqi society post-Saddam. . . . Dr. Chalabi and the other members of the seven-strong Iraqi opposition leadership were successfully positioned as authoritative political leaders." The effort was so successful, *PR Week* noted in the aftermath of Saddam's overthrow, that "the INC is now preparing to take over the role of interim authority in Iraq."[9]

If not for the terrorist attacks of September 11, 2001, however, things might have turned out differently. Under President Clinton, the CIA and State Department had formed a negative view of the INC and declined to disburse some of the funding approved by Congress. Once George W. Bush ascended to the presidency, Chalabi and the INC had guaranteed funding and well-positioned friends in the White House and Pentagon, though questions persisted. In early 2001, Chalabi appeared on the surface to be blowing his second chance as an Iraqi opposition leader. "Despite millions of dollars in U.S. aid," the *Los Angeles Times* reported in March of that year, "the leading Iraqi opposition group has proved so hapless in making use of the money, accounting for it, finding recruits for Pentagon training and preventing its own fragmentation that the State Department is searching for alternatives." The INC was described as "the gang that couldn't shoot straight," with "no meaningful support left inside Iraq and even less ability to threaten, much less topple, Saddam Hussein." Chalabi himself was called a "limousine insurgent," an "armchair guerrilla with homes in Georgetown and London."[10]

The INC had racked up big bills for PR and lavish accommodations on the State Department's tab with little to show for it. Its propaganda impact inside Iraq was minimal at best. Some $10 million had gone to pay for Liberty TV, a short-lived satellite television program produced by INC that went off the air in May 2002 amid questions about its management practices and lack of evidence that anyone inside Iraq was actually watching it. The INC also had a newspaper, *Al Mutamar*, but inside Iraq it was available only on the Internet, which most Iraqis were unable to access. The INC's poor bookkeeping also prompted a State Department audit that criticized $2.2 million of the $4.3 million in funding it received from the U.S. government between March 2000 and May 2001. Questionable items, according to the audit, included $2,070 to pay for membership at a Washington, D.C., health club, money paid to the Burson-Marsteller public relations firm, and lack of documentation for

$101,762 spent on participation at a human-rights conference. One of the INC's programs in particular drew criticism: its Information Collection Program, which incurred $465,940 in expenses that the auditor deemed "unsupported because of inadequate or a lack of documentation."[11] The Information Collection Program was supposed to support INC field officers stationed in countries surrounding Iraq, where their mission was to contact Iraq dissidents inside the country and collect information on the activities of Saddam Hussein's regime.[12] It was hard to see how a gym membership in Washington helped advance this mission. A more fundamental problem, which was not noted in the audit reports, is that the Information Collection Program effectively turned the Iraqi National Congress—a front group created by a public relations firm, with a strong desire to shape public opinion and policies—into a rogue intelligence agency, with a slush fund of vaguely monitored money that it could use to reward informants willing to say things that would serve its agenda.

American fears in the wake of September 11 presented a new opportunity, which the INC skillfully exploited. To sell a war with Iraq, Chalabi's people realized that it was essential to link Iraq somehow with Al Qaeda. To make the link, Brooke recalled later, "I sent out an all-points bulletin to our network, saying, 'Look, guys, get me a terrorist, or someone who works with terrorists. And, if you can get stuff on WMD, send it!'"[13] Until then, the INC's defectors had been providing information that helped prime the pump for more funding from Washington—reports on Iraq's human-rights abuses, or claims that the INC itself could topple the regime if only Congress would approve more money. In short order, the INC produced a series of new defectors saying that Iraq was working with Al Qaeda and preparing to supply terrorists with weapons of mass destruction.

The Information Collection Program also began arranging interviews directly between its defectors and American journalists. The extent of the manipulation was recorded by the INC itself, in a classified memo sent by INC spokesman Entifadh Qanbar to the U.S. Senate Appropriations Committee in June 2002. The memo remained unknown to the public until December 2003, when it was uncovered by reporters at *Newsweek* and subsequently described in detail by reporters Jonathan Landay and Tish Wells at the Knight Ridder news agency.

"The former Iraqi exile group that gave the Bush administration exaggerated and fabricated intelligence on Iraq also fed much of the same information to leading newspapers, news agencies and magazines in the United States, Britain and Australia," Landay and Wells concluded. Qanbar's memo listed 108 news stories containing information fed to journalists during a five-month period beginning in October 2001. The news stories based on INC-supplied information appeared in outlets including the *Atlantic Monthly*, New York *Daily News*, *New York Times*, *The New Yorker*, *Newsweek*, *Time*, *Washington Post*, *USA Today*, *Vanity Fair*, UPI, CBS television's *60 Minutes*, Fox News, the *Times* of London, and the *Sunday Age* of Melbourne, Australia. "The assertions in the articles," noted Landay and Wells, "reinforced President Bush's claims that Saddam Hussein should be ousted because he was in league with Osama bin Laden, was developing nuclear weapons and was hiding biological and chemical weapons. Feeding the information to the news media, as well as to selected administration officials and members of Congress, helped foster an impression that there were multiple sources of intelligence on Iraq's illicit weapons programs and links to bin Laden."[14]

The Dogs of War

In November 2001, *New York Times* reporter Chris Hedges published a story based on interviews with three INC-supplied defectors: Sabah Khalifa Khodada Alami, a former captain in the Iraqi army; an unnamed "former Iraqi sergeant"; and Abu Zeinab al-Qurairy, a former Iraqi lieutenant general and senior officer in Iraq's intelligence service. The defectors claimed that they had worked at Salman Pak, a top-secret Iraqi military facility located fifteen miles south of Baghdad. Their duties, they said, included training Islamic militants in terrorist techniques that included hijacking aircraft. Sabah Khodada went so far as to claim that the 9/11 operation "was conducted by people who were trained by Saddam."[15]

The claims by these same defectors were also featured in a *Washington Post* column by Jim Hoagland and a *Frontline* documentary aired later that week by the Public Broadcasting Service. A couple of months later, the same defectors were the basis for a lengthy article by David Rose for *Vanity Fair* magazine. In the *Vanity Fair* piece, al-Qurairy said he had worked closely with Saddam Hussein's son Uday in building a team of some 1,200 commandos called "the strikers." Some of them, he said, had left the country using false passports and were somewhere in the West preparing to wreak havoc. During three days of interviews, al-Qurairy regaled Rose with colorful, detailed stories that sounded like a plot for *Mission: Impossible*. As part of the training, al-Qurairy said, terrorists had to "land three helicopters on the roof of a speeding train on Salman Pak's own railroad, and then hijack it." Trainees who failed, he said, were "used as targets in live ammunition exercises." One of the other defectors described a training exercise in which they had to catch dogs "with our bare hands and kill them with our teeth, by biting the arteries in their necks."

As fantastic as these stories might seem, Rose believed them all, noting that al-Qurairy's INC handlers said they "had debriefed him thoroughly, checking every aspect of his story with sources inside Iraq and with other defectors. There was no doubt he was what he claimed. Before we met him, he had spent three days in Ankara, Turkey, with agents from the FBI and CIA. A senior CIA analyst told me that, as far as the agency was concerned, al-Qurairy was telling the truth."[16] Rose went on to write several subsequent stories based on INC-supplied information, including a glowing profile of Chalabi that praised his charisma, fearlessness, and "the unusual force of his intellect," and called him "the man who could save Iraq."[17]

Like many of the stories told by INC-supplied defectors, these claims have not survived the reality test. After occupying Iraq, U.S. forces visited the Salman Pak facility and did not find a railroad where anyone could have been practicing helicopter landings on speeding trains (assuming that there were actually terrorists stupid enough to prefer this method of boarding over the usual technique of simply buying a ticket). After other INC-supplied stories also unraveled, David Rose would conclude in 2004 that he had fallen victim to a misinformation campaign, for which he felt "profound regret."[18] He went on to become an outspoken journalistic critic of the propaganda used to sell the war, calling it a "campaign marked by miscalculation, bullying, and deception."[19]

In early 2006, the *Frontline* interviews could still be found on the PBS website, although editors added a note that said, "More than two years after the U.S.-led invasion of Iraq, there has been no verification of the general's account of the activities at Salman Pak. In fact, U.S. officials have now concluded that Salman Pak was most likely used to train Iraqi counter-terrorism units in anti-hijacking techniques." Moreover, the note continued, Abu Zeinab al-Qurairy "reportedly now lives in Baghdad; he claims not to have left Iraq before the fall of Saddam Hussein and that the story of Salman Pak was a hoax. He maintains that the man *Frontline* and the *New York Times* interviewed was an impostor provided by the INC."[20] Jack Fairweather, the former Baghdad bureau chief for the British *Daily Telegraph*, investigated the tale of the two al-Qurairys, and interviewed former INC members who told him that the man interviewed by *Frontline* and other journalists was actually "a former Iraqi sergeant, then living in Turkey and known by the code name Abu Zainab," whose military background helped add verisimilitude to the hoax.[21]

Investigative reporter Seymour Hersh also looked into the reports of terrorist training at Salman Pak, which does at least contain the shell of an airplane—not a Boeing 707, as the defectors claimed, but a Russian-built Tupolev 154. Hersh interviewed a former CIA station chief and a former military intelligence analyst, who told him that the Salman Pak facility was actually built in the 1980s with help from MI6, the British spy agency. "In the mid-eighties," Hersh explained, "Islamic terrorists were routinely hijacking aircraft. In 1986, an Iraqi airliner was seized by pro-Iranian extremists and crashed, after a hand grenade was triggered, killing at least sixty-five people. (At the time, Iran and Iraq were at war, and America favored Iraq.) Iraq then sought assistance from the West, and got what it wanted. . . . Inspectors recalled seeing the body of an airplane—which appeared to be used for counter-terrorism training—when they visited a biological-weapons facility near Salman Pak in 1991, ten years before September 11th. It is, of course, possible for such a camp to be converted from one purpose to another. The former CIA official noted, however, that terrorists would not practice on airplanes in the open. 'That's Hollywood rinky-dink stuff,' the former agent said. 'They train in basements. You don't need a real airplane to practice hijacking. The 9/11 terrorists went to gyms. But to take one back you have to practice on the real thing.' "[22]

A postwar review of the evidence by the Senate Intelligence Committee reached similar conclusions, describing the Salman Pak facility as "an unconventional warfare training facility used by the [Iraqi Intelligence Service] and Saddam Hussein's Fedayeen troops to train its officers for counterterrorism operations against regime opponents. The facility contained a village mockup for urban combat training and a derelict commercial aircraft." As for the claims made by the INC's defectors, the committee found that one of them "had embellished and exaggerated his access," while "other sources only repeated information provided by the [first] defector, and also lacked first-hand access to the information. Committee staff asked both CIA and DIA analysts whether any al-Qaida operatives or other sources have confirmed Salman Pak training allegations, and the unanimous response was that none have reported knowledge of any training."[23]

Notwithstanding the official debunking of the Salman Pak claims, they continue to circulate widely. A Google search in February 2006 for the phrase "Salman Pak" returned 109,000 hits. Of the top fifty, more than half recounted the allegations made by the INC's defectors, with only a handful of mentions that these claims have been investigated and refuted. The idea that Salman Pak was a training ground for Al Qaeda continued to circulate in right-wing publications such as the *Weekly Standard*, which featured an article in January 2006 by Stephen Hayes claiming that "documents and photographs recovered by the U.S. military in postwar Iraq" prove that Saddam Hussein's region "trained thousands of radical Islamic terrorists from the region at camps in Iraq over the four years immediately preceding the U.S. invasion." Although Hayes had not actually *seen* any of the "documents and photographs" in question, he insisted that if only the U.S. government would release them publicly, they would support his point.[24]

Curveball's Sliders

The INC also played a role in promoting one of the most sensational claims about Iraq's alleged weapons of mass destruction—the claim that it had developed "mobile production facilities"—rolling truck trailers to make biological weapons. In Colin Powell's prewar speech to the United Nations, he called the mobile weapons labs "one of the most worrisome things that emerges from the thick intelligence file we have on Iraq's biological weapons." The information, he said, came from "an eyewitness, an Iraqi chemical engineer who supervised one of these facilities," and had been confirmed by three other sources who provided "highly detailed and extremely accurate" descriptions of fermentors, pumps, tanks and compressors, and other components used in the labs.

It is now known that the "Iraqi chemical engineer" mentioned by Powell was an Iraq defector debriefed by Germany's intelligence service and never interviewed directly by the United States. The Germans regarded him as mentally unstable, alcoholic, and "out of control" and code-named him "Curveball"—an indication of the skepticism they felt toward his claims. They conveyed these doubts in forceful terms to the United States, stating on one occasion, "Don't even ask to see him because he's a fabricator and he's crazy."[25] The Silberman-Robb report, written by the commission appointed by President Bush to investigate intelligence failures leading up to the war, noted that "serious concerns about Curveball were widely known at CIA in the months leading up to Secretary Powell's speech," but says it is "unclear precisely how and why these serious concerns about Curveball never reached Secretary Powell."[26]

This mystery becomes perhaps less mysterious if you consider how intelligence analysts were treated when they did raise concerns. According to the Silberman-Robb report, "One analyst, after presenting his case in late 2003 that Curveball had fabricated his reporting, was 'read the riot act' by his office director, who accused him of 'making waves' and being 'biased.' The analyst told Commission staff that he was subsequently asked to leave WINPAC" (the CIA's weapons proliferation unit, where Valerie Plame Wilson also worked). The Silberman-Robb report notes that another WINPAC chemical weapons analyst "who pressed to publish a reassessment of Iraq's [chemical weapons] program in late 2003 was also, according to the analysts, 'told to leave' WINPAC."[27] Although there were wide doubts about Curveball, his claim that Iraq was using mobile weapons laboratories to elude inspectors appeared in more than one hundred U.S. government reports. When one agent raised questions about the reliability of Curveball's information, he received an e-mail from the deputy of the CIA Counter Proliferation Unit, who shot down the objections, not because they were unfounded but because they might undermine the case for war. The e-mail, which was sent a day before Colin Powell's UN appearance, admonished the agent to "keep in mind the fact that this war's going to happen regardless of what Curve Ball said or didn't say and that the Powers That Be probably aren't terribly interested in whether Curve Ball knows what he's talking about."[28]

The Silberman-Robb report also found a remarkable pattern

of amnesia among top CIA officials, who declared themselves unable to recall ever hearing questions raised about Curveball, although their subordinates were equally adamant in remembering heated discussions about his general unreliability and the fact that satellite photographs and other evidence contradicted his descriptions of sites he claimed to have visited. "The fact is there was yelling and screaming about this guy. . . . My people were saying: 'We think he's a stinker,'" said James L. Pavitt, who was the CIA's deputy director of operations at the time. Tyler Drumheller, the former chief of the CIA European Division, said he personally discussed Curveball with top officials including John McLaughlin, the chief deputy to CIA director George Tenet. "Everyone in the chain of command knew exactly what was happening," said Drumheller, scoffing at claims by Tenet and McLauglin that they were unaware of concerns about Curveball's credibility. "They can say whatever they want," Drumheller said. "They know what the truth is. . . . I did not lie." He added that "there are literally inches and inches of documentation" including "dozens and dozens of e-mails and memos and things like that detailing meetings" where officials sharply questioned Curveball's credibility.[29]

Faced with the CIA's inability to provide a coherent account of what its own intelligence analysts knew or said, the Silberman-Robb report basically threw up its hands and refused to draw conclusions. "This Commission was not established to adjudicate personal responsibility for the intelligence errors on Iraq," it stated. "We are not an adjudicatory body, nor did we take testimony under oath. We were not authorized or equipped to assign blame to specific individuals, particularly when there are disputes about critical facts." Nevertheless, it somehow managed to declare, "There was no 'politicization' of the intelligence product on Iraq."[30]

The Silberman-Robb report also managed to provide some exoneration for the Iraqi National Congress with respect to the Curveball affair. The *Los Angeles Times* reported in 2004 that Curveball was actually the brother of one of Ahmed Chalabi's bodyguards, and the *New York Times* reported that Curveball was introduced to German intelligence by the INC.[31] The INC itself, however, denied that it directed Curveball, and Silberman-Robb stated that "the CIA's post-war investigations were unable to uncover any evidence that the INC or any other organization was directing Curveball to feed misleading information to the Intelligence Community."[32] Even if this is true, however, another defector supplied by the INC, Mohamed Harith, *did* provide similar information. Harith was one of the other sources cited by Colin Powell in his United Nations speech as "corroboration" for Curveball's claims—even though the CIA concluded that he, too, had fabricated his claims.

The Silberman-Robb report also concluded that "INC-related sources had a minimal impact on pre-war assessments" by the CIA,[33] but this conclusion comes with a big caveat. In fact, there were heated debates within the intelligence community about INC-supplied information, with White House officials such as Dick Cheney and Scooter Libby apparently preferring unfiltered information that they received directly from the INC over the more cautious formal assessments provided by CIA analysts. In addition to appearing in Colin Powell's speech to the United Nations, the INC's false information popped up in President Bush's own speech to the UN on September 12, 2002, as well as in a White House–prepared paper on Saddam Hussein's alleged weapons of mass destruction and links to terrorism titled A *Decade of Deception and Defiance*. As we have detailed above, INC sources also played a big role in prewar news coverage through defectors who took their stories directly to the media. In addition to influencing Powell's speech, Mohamed Harith was a source for a story published by David Rose for *Vanity Fair* and a March 2002 interview with Lesley Stahl on CBS's *60 Minutes*. White House statements and news stories that relied on INC informants were not formal "pre-war assessments" by the U.S. intelligence community, but they played a significant role in shaping public opinion and selling the war.

Miller Time

The collapse of the administration's claims about Iraqi WMDs also prompted scrutiny of reports written for the *New York Times* by Judith Miller. During the eighteen months leading up to the war, Miller had published a series of sensational stories with headlines such as "CIA Hunts Iraq Tie to Soviet Smallpox," "U.S. Experts Find Radioactive Material in Iraq," and "Iraq Said to Try to Buy Antidote Against Nerve Gas." Several of her reports relied on tips and sources provided by the Iraqi National Congress.

➤ "Iraqi Tells of Renovations at Sites for Chemical and Nuclear Arms," published on December 20, 2001, told the story of Adnan Ihsan Saeed al-Haideri, a defector provided by the INC who said he had personally visited and worked on the construction of at least twenty secret weapons facilities for biological, chemical, and nuclear weapons. The secret sites, he said, were "hidden in the rear of government companies and private villas in residential areas, or underground in what were built to look like water wells which are lined with lead-filled concrete and contain no water." Another hidden laboratory, he said, had been built underground, directly underneath Saddam Hussein Hospital, the largest hospital in Baghdad. Miller reported his claims, adding, "The experts said his information seemed reliable and significant."[34] In fact, three days before being interviewed by Miller, al-Haideri had failed a polygraph test administered by the CIA. His claims were nevertheless featured prominently in White House statements and intelligence briefings. Two years later, after Saddam Hussein was removed from power, the Iraq Survey Group brought him back to Iraq so that he could personally point out the weapons sites where he had worked. He was unable to point out a single site associated with banned weapons.[35]

➤ "U.S. Says Hussein Intensifies Quest for A-Bomb Parts," published on September 8, 2002, repeated administration claims that Iraq was seeking aluminum tubes for use in producing nuclear weapons. It also quoted another Iraqi defector, who used the pseudonym "Ahmed al-Shemri" and who spoke only on condition that Miller not identify even the country in which he was interviewed. "All of Iraq is one large storage facility" for deadly chemical agents, he told her, stating that Saddam had stockpiled "12,500 gallons of anthrax, 2,500 gallons of gas gangrene, 1,250 gallons of aflatoxin, and 2,000 gallons of botulinum throughout the country."[36] None of these claims have ever been corroborated, and no one has heard anything since from Ahmed al-Shemri.

➤ "White House Lists Iraq Steps to Build Banned Weapons," published on September 13, 2002, quoted White House charges that Iraq possessed mobile laboratories to make biological weapons as well as ingredients to make poison gas. It also repeated the administration's claims about aluminum tubes, citing unnamed "senior officials" who "said it was the intelligence agencies' unanimous view" that the tubes Iraq was seeking were for centrifuges to extract uranium for nuclear weapons. (In fact, there was already visible disagreement within the U.S. intelligence community about whether the tubes were for centrifuges or for artillery rockets in Iraq's military program.)[37]

➤ "Verification Is Difficult at Best, Say the Experts, and Maybe Impossible," published on September 18, 2002, questioned the effectiveness of UNMOVIC and chief weapons inspector Hans Blix and also gave credence to statements by Khidhir Hamza, another Iraqi defector who resettled in the United States with help from the Iraqi National Congress. Hamza was the author of a book titled *Saddam's Bombmaker* in which he claimed that he led

Iraq's nuclear bomb program prior to his defection. He told Miller that Iraq was at the "pilot plant" stage of nuclear production and within two to three years of mass-producing centrifuges to enrich uranium for a bomb.[38] Hamza's stories have also failed the reality test. Hussein Kamel, Saddam Hussein's son-in-law, who was later killed by the regime as punishment for his defection to the West, described Hamza as "a professional liar" when he was interrogated by Western arm investigators. Former United Nations weapons inspector David Albright remembers that the original title of Hamza's book was *Fizzle: Iraq and the Atomic Bomb*. In its original version, it described how Iraq had *failed* in its effort to develop nuclear weapons in the 1980s. After he was unable to find a publisher for the original manuscript, Hamza reworked it into a book that reached the opposite conclusion and found a ready audience.[39]

➤ "U.S. Faulted Over Its Efforts to Unite Iraqi Dissidents," published on October 2, 2002, read like a class reunion for INC defectors. It featured complaints by al-Haideri, Hamza, and Ahmed Chalabi to the effect that the CIA was not listening to them enough. It cited similar sentiments from Pentagon adviser Richard Perle along with Danielle Pletka of the American Enterprise Institute, a conservative Washington think tank that was also a fan of the INC. Perle praised the INC as "the single most important source of intelligence about Saddam Hussein," while Pletka complained: "The treatment of Iraqi opposition figures and the lack of a coherent policy towards them is an utter disgrace."[40]

Many of Miller's stories were reprinted or cited by other news media around the world, reflecting the special role that the *New York Times* plays within the ecosystem of American journalism. Nicknamed the Gray Lady, it is often referred to as the "newspaper of record" in the United States. By virtue of its age, its large readership, and its often-deserved reputation for careful, high-quality reporting, the *Times* tends to set the tone for other publications. In addition to its prestige, it plays another role as ideological gatekeeper. Conservatives in the United States have frequently accused the paper of having a "liberal bias." This claim is debatable, but it helps define the *New York Times* as the "left end" of acceptable political discourse. The front-page play given to Judith Miller's reporting therefore played a significant role in shaping public perceptions. If even the *New York Times* reported that Iraq possessed hidden WMDs, a large number of other journalists, and a correspondingly broad cross-section of the American public, were bound to conclude that it must be true.

In one story, written two months before the start of war, Miller noted that "former Iraqi scientists, military officers and contractors"—the defectors on whom her own reporting had heavily relied—"have provided American intelligence agencies with a portrait of Saddam Hussein's secret programs to develop and conceal chemical, biological and nuclear weapons that is starkly at odds with the findings so far of the United Nations weapons inspectors."[41] In Miller's hands, this stark difference seemed to suggest that the UN inspectors were naive or incompetent. Once the United States occupied Iraq, however, the word of her sources turned out to be starkly at odds with reality itself.

Embedded with the Military

After Iraq came under American control, Miller became an embedded reporter with Mobile Exploitation Team Alpha, one of the units of the 75th Exploitation Task Force charged with finding weapons of mass destruction. Her role with MET Alpha seems to have gone beyond the normal role expected of a journalist. *Washington Post* media writer Howard Kurtz reported that her actions prompted complaints from soldiers who said she had turned MET Alpha into a "rogue operation," using her clout to influence its activities and priorities. "More than a half-dozen military officers said that Miller acted as a middleman between the Army unit with which she was embedded and Iraqi National Congress leader Ahmed Chalabi, on one occasion accompanying Army officers to Chalabi's headquarters, where they took custody of Saddam Hussein's son-in-law," Kurtz wrote. "She also sat in on the initial debriefing of the son-in-law." This upset other military officials because the MET Alpha team was not trained in effective interrogation techniques. According to one officer, "She was leading them. . . . She ended up almost hijacking the mission."[42]

Kurtz also reported on leaked e-mail correspondence that he had received between Miller and John Burns, the Baghdad bureau chief for the *Times*. The e-mail detailed a clash between the two journalists that occurred when Miller wrote a profile of Chalabi without clearing it with Burns first. Burns sent her an e-mail complaining that she had upstaged another correspondent who was working on a separate profile of Chalabi. Burns said he was "deeply chagrined" that she had done so, "after I had told you on Monday night that we were planning a major piece on him—and without so much as telling me what you were doing. We have a bureau here; I am in charge of that bureau until I leave; I make assignments after considerable thought and discussion, and it was plain to all of us to whom the Chalabi story belonged. If you do this, what is to stop you doing it on any other story of your choosing? And what of the distress it causes the correspondent who is usurped? It is not professional, and not collegial."

Miller replied: "I've been covering Chalabi for about ten years, and have done most of the stories about him for our paper, including the long takeout we recently did on him. He has provided most of the front page exclusives on WMD to our paper." She added that her MET Alpha unit "is using Chalabi's intell [sic] and document network for its own WMD work. . . . I'm there every day, talking to him."[43]

The result of this collaboration was a string of Judith Miller exclusives with headlines such as "U.S. Analysts Link Iraq Labs to Germ Arms," "Radioactive Material Found at a Test Site Near Baghdad," "Trailer Is a Mobile Lab Capable of Turning Out Bioweapons," and "U.S. Aides Say Iraqi Truck Could Be a Germ-War Lab." Perhaps her most sensational (and later notorious) report was an April 21 filing in which she breathlessly reported that an Iraqi scientist had "led Americans to a supply of material that proved to be the building blocks of illegal weapons, which he claimed to have buried as evidence of Iraq's illicit weapons programs."

How were these claims confirmed? In her story, Miller admitted that she had not been told the name of the scientist or allowed to interview him, nor was she allowed to mention what chemicals had been discovered. She was also forbidden "to write about the discovery of the scientist for three days, and the copy was then submitted for a check by military officials." However, she was "permitted to see him from a distance at the sites where he said that material from the arms program was buried. Clad in nondescript clothes and a baseball cap, he pointed to several spots in the sand where he said chemical precursors and other weapons material were buried." All she actually saw, in other words, was some guy in a baseball cap—with whom she was not allowed to speak—standing at a distance and pointing at the ground. Nevertheless, the story ran on page one of the *New York Times*. It quoted a U.S. general saying that the guy in the baseball cap "could prove to be of incalculable value. . . . [I]f it proves out it will clearly be one of the major discoveries of this operation, and it may be the major discovery."[44]

Miller's story was so vague about specifics and so thinly sourced that other reporters at the *Times* grumbled to *New York Observer* reporter Sridhar Pappu about the decision to run it at all. One source at the *Times* called it "wacky-assed."[45] Three months later, Miller would admit, without elaboration, that the "man who originally identified himself as a scientist . . . turned out to be a military intelligence officer."[46] What other lies had he told? No one knows. A year later, in a public mea culpa, editors at the *New York Times* would admit only that the *Times* "never followed up on the veracity of this source or the attempts to verify his claims."[47]

In another story, Miller reported that "American-led forces

have occupied a vast warehouse complex in Baghdad filled with chemicals where Iraqi scientists are suspected of having tested unconventional agents on dogs." Although she herself "was not permitted to visit the warehouse," she "heard descriptions of it from Americans who went to the location."[48] No one has written anything further about the warehouse, and given the vagueness of Miller's description, no one else ever can.

Avoidance of specifics is a common characteristic of propaganda, which seeks to instill a desired attitude in its target audience while avoiding careful scrutiny of the actual facts behind its claims. Miller's reporting on Iraq was unusually full of vague details and also anonymous sources, who were variously described as "senior Bush officials," "an official," "experts," "an informant whose identity has not been disclosed," "dissidents," "Iraqi defectors," "intelligence officials," "an elite American team," "weapons experts," and so forth. There are, of course, some circumstances in which people genuinely need to speak anonymously to a reporter, but in retrospect it is clear that many of Miller's sources chose anonymity so they could avoid being held personally accountable for statements which later turned out to be lies. Eventually, the lies became obvious. At *Slate* magazine, editor Jack Schafer, who had supported the war with Iraq, became increasingly incensed at the gap between what he had read in the *Times* and what was unfolding on the ground. In a blistering commentary titled "The *Times* Scoops That Melted," he wrote in July 2003, "If reporters who live by their sources were obliged to die by their sources," Miller "would be stinking up her family tomb right now."[49]

The *Times* admitted that it was receiving a deluge of e-mail and letters criticizing the paper's coverage but responded initially with a blanket refusal to investigate. *Times* executive editor Bill Keller defended Miller in March 2004 as "smart, well-sourced, industrious and fearless" and said he "did not see a prima facie case for recanting or repudiating the stories. The brief against the coverage was that it was insufficiently skeptical, but that is an easier claim to make in hindsight than in context. . . . [L]acking prima facie evidence, opening a docket and litigating the claims against the coverage was likely to consume more of my attention than I was willing to invest."[50]

In May 2004, the paper even took the Bush administration to task for relying on a "questionable character" like Ahmed Chalabi—without acknowledging that its own reporting had relied heavily on Chalabi and other INC sources. In fact, it took the *New York Times* even longer than the Bush administration to admit that its intelligence on Iraq was flawed. The *Times* waited eighteen months, as questions and criticisms multiplied, before finally issuing a carefully phrased admission that its reporting on Iraq included "a number of instances of coverage that was not as rigorous as it should have been" and "sometimes fell for misinformation." The self-critique, which nowhere mentioned Judith Miller by name, noted that the not-as-rigorous-as-it-should-have-been reporting consisted of stories that "shared a common feature. They depended at least in part on information from a circle of Iraqi informants, defectors and exiles bent on 'regime change' in Iraq, people whose credibility has come under increasing public debate in recent weeks."[51]

A second assessment, by *Times* ombudsman Daniel Okrent, went a bit further: "The failure was not individual, but institutional," Okrent wrote. "War requires an extra standard of care, not a lesser one. But in the *Times*'s WMD coverage, readers encountered some rather breathless stories built on unsubstantiated 'revelations' that, in many instances, were the anonymity-cloaked assertions of people with vested interests. *Times* reporters broke many stories before and after the war—but when the stories themselves later broke apart, in many instances *Times* readers never found out. . . . Other stories pushed Pentagon assertions so aggressively you could almost sense epaulets sprouting on the shoulders of editors."[52]

Paradoxically, the "Plamegate" scandal that we described in chapter two provided Judith Miller with a measure of redemption in the eyes of some of her journalistic colleagues. Miller was one of the reporters approached by Scooter Libby, Dick Cheney's chief of staff, during the White House whispering campaign against Joseph and Valerie Plame Wilson. After the leak of Mrs. Wilson's identity as a covert CIA agent became a target of investigation by federal prosecutor Patrick Fitzgerald, Miller was asked to testify but refused, based on her journalistic pledge to defend the confidentiality of her source. A judge found her in contempt of court and sent her to jail for eighty-five days. The *New York Times* editorialized on her behalf, as did many other journalists. CNN's Lou Dobbs called her jailing "an onerous, disgusting abuse of government power." Reporters Without Borders called it "a dark day for freedom of the press." Upon her release, the Society of Professional Journalists gave her its First Amendment Award.

The solidarity ended, however, after Miller received a waiver from Libby and testified to a grand jury about their conversations. The testimony revealed things that her own editors at the

Times had not known, and resentment from other reporters bub-
bled to a boil. In a message to staffers, Keller admitted that "wait-
ing a year to own up to our mistakes . . . allowed the anger inside
and outside the paper to fester. Worse, we fear, we fostered an
impression that the *Times* put a higher premium on protecting
its reporters than on coming clean with its readers. If we had
lanced the WMD boil earlier, we might have damped any suspicion that *this* time, the paper was putting the defense of a reporter above the duty to its readers." Keller added that Miller
had apparently withheld information from *Times* Washington
bureau chief Phil Taubman. "Until Fitzgerald came after her,"
Keller stated, "I didn't know that Judy had been one of the reporters on the receiving end of the anti-Wilson whisper campaign. I should have wondered why I was learning this from the
special counsel, a year after the fact. (In November of 2003, Phil
Taubman tried to ascertain whether any of our correspondents
had been offered similar leaks. . . . Judy seems to have misled
Phil Taubman about the extent of her involvement.)"[53]

Miller's testimony also revealed something that former CBS
News correspondent Bill Lynch called an "enormous journalism scandal."[54] Under the terms of her unusual Department of
Defense security clearance while she was an embedded journalist, Miller said, she was allowed "to see secret information." During her conversation with Libby, she said, "I might have
expressed frustration to Mr. Libby that I was not permitted to discuss with editors some of the more sensitive information about
Iraq."[55]

An arrangement of this sort might be acceptable if Miller
were an intelligence operative for the U.S. government, but as a

journalist, her first obligation should have been her readers' right to know. Instead, she was working under terms that forbade her to disclose what she knew even to her editors, let alone to the public at large. "This is as close as one can get to government licensing of journalists," Lynch wrote, "and the *New York Times* (if it knew) should never have allowed her to become so compromised."[56]

Miller's uncommon security clearance casts another light on her decision to protect Scooter Libby as her anonymous source in the Plamegate affair. Originally, the *Times* and other publications defended her refusal to testify as a matter of journalistic principle. But whom was she protecting with her refusal, if not the most powerful officials in the government itself?

A core tenet of journalism is that reporters protect their sources so they can better serve the public's right to know the truth. They must talk to anonymous sources, the tenet holds, so that they can unearth facts from whistleblowers and other people who might otherwise fear retaliation from the powerful for speaking out. In Miller's case, however, the formula was inverted: her sources were the powerful, using anonymity to shield their identities so they could deceive the public and punish a whistleblower. At what point does a reporter cease to be an independent journalist and become instead a covert agent for the government itself and a purveyor of government propaganda? Judith Miller and the *New York Times* may have crossed that line.

That Was Then, This Is Now

By the time the *New York Times* began to reconsider its reporting on Iraq, the Bush administration's own relationship with Ahmed Chalabi and the Iraqi National Congress had soured dramatically. Following the toppling of Saddam Hussein, the U.S. had given Chalabi one of the twenty-five seats on its hand-picked new Iraqi Governing Council. The White House was irked, however, when Chalabi gave an interview to the London *Daily Telegraph* in which he tacitly acknowledged that his network of informants had provided false information. "We are heroes in error," he said. "As far as we're concerned we've been entirely successful. That tyrant Saddam is gone and the Americans are in Baghdad. What was said before is not important."[57]

By the spring of 2004, U.S. intelligence analysts began to realize that Chalabi had used another technique to further game the system. Relying on the fact that even friendly spy services rarely share the identities of their informants, the INC created an "echo chamber" effect by sending defectors to Denmark, England, Italy, France, Germany, Spain, and Sweden as well as the United States. As a result, U.S. intelligence analysts used information from "foreign intelligence sources" to corroborate their own assessments, without realizing that their corroboration was also coming from the INC. "We had a lot of sources, but it was all coming from the same pot," said a former senior U.S. intelligence official. "They were all INC guys. And none of them panned out."[58]

Once in Iraq, Chalabi's political alliances also changed. His neoconservative backers in the United States had imagined that he would support secularism and friendly relations with Israel. Based on INC-supplied intelligence and promises from Chalabi, U.S. officials had even promoted plans for a trade treaty that would reestablish direct sales and shipments of oil from Iraq to Israel—including reconstruction of an oil pipeline that had been dismantled and abandoned ever since Israel's declaration of independence in 1948.[59] Instead, Chalabi developed an alliance with Shiite fundamentalists inside Iraq and supported a boycott of Israel, staking out positions in line with the country's political realities. In retrospect, argued financial columnist John Dizard in *Salon*, Chalabi's earlier promises looked like strategic deceptions aimed at hornswoggling the neocons into backing the war. Political realities inside Iraq, he said, would never have tolerated a pro-Israel tilt: "The Shia community in Iraq, like the Sunni community, is overwhelmingly anti-Israel, and the entire range of its leadership has close ties with Iran. . . . Chalabi appears to have recognized that the neocons, while ruthless, realistic and effective in bureaucratic politics, were remarkably ignorant about the situation in Iraq, and willing to buy a fantasy of how the country's politics worked. So he sold it to them."[60]

U.S. intelligence officials became increasingly suspicious about Chalabi's relationship with Iran, where the INC maintained an office and he made regular visits for meetings with top government leaders. The Pentagon's $335,000 monthly payments to the INC's Information Collection Program continued until May 2004, when American troops raided Chalabi's headquarters and home in Baghdad, arrested two of his aides, and seized documents. According to *Newsweek*, "Bush administration officials have been briefed on intelligence indicating that Chalabi and some of his top aides have supplied Iran with 'sensitive' information on the American occupation in Iraq. U.S. officials say that electronic intercepts of discussions between Iranian leaders indicate that Chalabi and his entourage told Iranian contacts about American political plans in Iraq. There are also indications that Chalabi has provided details of U.S. security operations. According to one U.S. government source, some of the information Chalabi turned over to Iran could 'get people killed.' "[61]

The raid on Chalabi's headquarters followed an FBI investigation that was launched after the United States intercepted a secret message from an Iranian intelligence agent in Baghdad who told his superiors that Chalabi had revealed that Americans had cracked Iran's encryption code. "The communication said a drunken American official gave Chalabi the information," reported Walter Pincus and Dana Priest in the *Washington Post*. Cracking the code had enabled the United States to monitor top-secret Iranian communiqués, but now that the Iranians knew their code was compromised, they were certain to take countermeasures. "In a closed-door damage assessment on Capitol Hill," wrote Pincus and Priest, "National Security Agency officials said the disclosure cut off a significant stream of information about Iran at a time when the United States is worried about the country's nuclear ambitions, its support for terrorist groups and its efforts to exert greater influence over Iraq."[62]

Only five months earlier, Chalabi had been a guest of honor

sitting right behind Laura Bush at the president's State of the Union address.

Faced with evidence of Chalabi's ties to Iran, some of his longtime supporters in the United States began to back away, while others, such as Danielle Pletka at the American Enterprise Institute, continued to defend him publicly. The Bush administration also moved to distance itself from the man who had once supplied some of the most sensational evidence used in making the case for war. However, they were unable to ignore him completely. Through a political alliance with Muqtada al-Sadr, the radical Shiite cleric whose militia battled U.S. troops in August 2004 in the Iraqi city of Najaf, Chalabi managed to get himself appointed deputy prime minister of Iraq in April 2005. In this capacity, he made an official visit to Washington in November of that year. The visit created an awkward moment for the Bush administration, which agreed to meet with him while also distancing itself from his past.

"Think of him as a former football player—that was all then. That's what he did in his other life," said a senior White House official, speaking (of course) on condition of anonymity.[63]

CHAPTER FIVE

Rewriting History

IN NOVEMBER 2005, PRESIDENT BUSH CHOSE VET-
erans' Day to lash out at "Democrats and anti-war critics" who
"are now claiming we manipulated the intelligence and misled
the American people about why we went to war." It was "deeply
irresponsible," Bush said, "to rewrite the history of how that war
began."[1]

The Bush administration itself, however, has tried repeatedly
to rewrite the history of the war. In July 2003, when his popularity was still high, Bush explained the justification for war
as follows, during a photo opportunity with United Nations

secretary-general Kofi Annan: "The fundamental question is, did Saddam Hussein have a weapons program? And the answer is, absolutely. And we gave him a chance to allow the inspectors in, and he wouldn't let them in. And therefore, after a reasonable request, we decided to remove him from power, along with other nations, so as to make sure he was not a threat to the United States and our friends and allies in the region."[2]

This was as clear a case of a falsehood as can be imagined. Weapons inspectors were not allowed to operate in Iraq during a four-year period beginning in 1999, but contrary to Bush's claim, Saddam Hussein *did* allow the weapons inspectors to return in 2002, and they were only withdrawn for their own safety when Bush decided to bypass them and the United Nations Security Council and proceed with his invasion of Iraq. Yet Bush's falsehood received barely a peep of criticism at the time from U.S. news media, still seemingly hypnotized by Bush's popularity. His statement was ignored altogether by the *New York Times*. The *Washington Post* noted the discrepancy between Bush's words and reality in the most polite terms possible, stating merely that "the president's assertion that the war began because Iraq did not admit inspectors appeared to contradict the events leading up to the war this spring: Hussein had, in fact, admitted the inspectors and Bush had opposed extending their work because he did not believe them effective."[3]

Since then, the administration's rhetoric about Iraq has shifted further, and the changes have taken it in directions that undermine its original case for war. During the initial buildup to war, the main arguments were:

- We know that Iraq has weapons of mass destruction.
- Saddam Hussein is allied with Al Qaeda.
- The people will welcome American troops as liberators, so the war will be a "cakewalk" and the postinvasion occupation will be brief.

These arguments have now shifted to the following:

- We were wrong about our intelligence assessments, but so was everyone else.
- We can't leave now, or the terrorists will win.
- If we leave now, all the lives and money we've spent will have been wasted.

Each of these arguments is also deceptive, but before considering the specifics of *how* they are misleading, it is worth noting that each of the current arguments is a pale and unconvincing version of the original case for war. The Bush administration has been forced to fall back on these weaker arguments because it has no choice. Reality is sinking in, even at the top levels of government.

Let's look at each of the Bush administration's current arguments in turn.

"We Were Wrong, but So Was Everybody Else"

It is true that many (though not all) analysts outside the White House expected that chemical or biological weapons would be found in Iraq, but there was little expectation that they would be found in the quantities that the Bush administration talked about or that they would constitute an imminent threat to the United States. With regard to a nuclear weapons program, however, there was considerably more skepticism about White House claims.

It is also true that many leading Democratic politicians supported the Bush administration's drive to war, but members of Congress did not have access to the same intelligence information as the White House. Congress received summaries, provided by the White House, from which the details and grounds for skepticism had been removed. By law, highly classified intelligence information is seen only by members of the Senate and House Intelligence Committtees, who are not allowed to share that information even with other members of Congress. Florida senator Bob Graham, who chaired the Senate Intelligence Committee in the months leading up to the war with Iraq, says he saw a disturbing difference between the information that he saw during that period and the public assessments that were shared with the public and the rest of Congress:

> At a meeting of the Senate intelligence committee on Sept. 5, 2002, CIA Director George Tenet was asked what the National Intelligence Estimate (NIE) provided as the rationale for a preemptive war in Iraq. An NIE is the product of the entire intelligence community, and its most comprehensive assessment. I was stunned when Tenet said that no NIE had been requested by the White House and none had been pre-

pared. Invoking our rarely used senatorial authority, I directed the completion of an NIE.

Tenet objected, saying that his people were too committed to other assignments to analyze Saddam Hussein's capabilities and will to use chemical, biological and possibly nuclear weapons. We insisted, and three weeks later the community produced a classified NIE.

There were troubling aspects to this 90-page document. While slanted toward the conclusion that Hussein possessed weapons of mass destruction stored or produced at 550 sites, it contained vigorous dissents on key parts of the information, especially by the departments of State and Energy. Particular skepticism was raised about aluminum tubes that were offered as evidence Iraq was reconstituting its nuclear program. As to Hussein's will to use whatever weapons he might have, the estimate indicated he would not do so unless he was first attacked. . . .

The American people needed to know these reservations, and I requested that an unclassified, public version of the NIE be prepared. On Oct. 4, Tenet presented a 25-page document titled "Iraq's Weapons of Mass Destruction Programs." It represented an unqualified case that Hussein possessed them, avoided a discussion of whether he had the will to use them and omitted the dissenting opinions contained in the classified version.[4]

The gap between what the White House knew and what it told the public is even wider than the gap between what it knew and what it told Congress—so wide that Congressman Henry

Waxman has compiled an online database, called *Iraq on the Record*, which lists 237 statements made by Bush, Cheney, Rice, Powell, or Rumsfeld which were false in light of intelligence reports known to the White House at the time the statements were made. Space, of course, does not allow us to list them all here, but to cite just one example, it quotes Bush and other officials saying that Iraq possessed "massive" stockpiles of biological and chemical weapons at a time when the October 2002 National Intelligence Estimate prepared by the CIA stated, "There is no reliable information on whether Iraq is producing and stockpiling chemical weapons or where Iraq has—or will—establish its chemical warfare agent production facilities."[5] With regard to biological weapons, the report said, "the size of those stockpiles is uncertain and is subject to debate. The nature and condition of those stockpiles also are unknown."[6]

It is also not the case, as the Bush administration has claimed, that intelligence estimates by other countries universally reached the same conclusions as the United States regarding Iraqi weapons of mass destruction or alleged links to terrorists. Here's what some of them said on the eve of war:

➤ "Fears are one thing, hard facts are another," said Russian president Vladimir Putin on October 11, 2002. "Russia does not have in its possession any trustworthy data that supports the existence of nuclear weapons or any weapons of mass destruction in Iraq and we have not received any such information from our partners as yet. This fact has also been supported by the information sent by the CIA to the US Congress."[7]

➤ "Nothing today justifies a war," said French president Jacques Chirac on February 11, 2003, adding that France did not have "undisputed proof" that Iraq still held weapons of mass destruction. Chirac made his remarks standing alongside Putin as they announced that France, Russia, and Germany had agreed on a joint declaration calling for an increase in the number of weapons inspectors as an "alternative to war."[8] According to CNN White House correspondent John King, Chirac's statement made Bush administration officials "apoplectic"—not because he was calling again for weapons inspectors to be given more time, but because he publicly challenged the administration's claim that Iraq had WMDs.[9]

➤ Arab nations also overwhelmingly rejected the Bush administration's case for war. In February 2003, the Arab League endorsed a resolution opposing "any assistance or facilities to any military operation that might threaten the security, safety, and territorial integrity of Iraq." The resolution was signed by representatives of all of the league's twenty-two member nations with the exception of Kuwait.[10]

Finally, of course, there are any number of commentators in the United States who questioned the case for war before it happened. The skeptics ranged across the political spectrum. Skeptics on the right included Patrick Buchanan and retired general William Odom (a former national security adviser to President Reagan).

Brent Scowcroft, the former national security adviser to the first president Bush, also publicly disagreed with the case for war presented by Bush the younger. In an August 2002 op-ed for the *Wall Street Journal*, Scowcroft wrote that "there is scant evidence to tie Saddam to terrorist organizations, and even less to the Sept. 11 attacks. Indeed Saddam's goals have little in common with the terrorists who threaten us, and there is little incentive for him to make common cause with them." Scowcroft accepted the administration's claim that Iraq possessed WMDs, but warned, "An attack on Iraq at this time would seriously jeopardize, if not destroy, the global counter-terrorist campaign we have undertaken. The United States could certainly defeat the Iraqi military and destroy Saddam's regime. But it would not be a cakewalk. On the contrary, it undoubtedly would be very expensive—with serious consequences for the U.S. and global economy—and could as well be bloody. . . . Finally, if we are to achieve our strategic objectives in Iraq, a military campaign very likely would have to be followed by a large-scale, long-term military occupation."[11]

In an interview with Fox News, Lawrence Eagleburger, who had served as secretary of state for the senior Bush, expressed similar sentiments. "I'm scared to death," he said, "that the Richard Perles and the Wolfowitzes of this world are arguing that we can do it in a cakewalk, when I think it will take some hundreds of thousands of troops at least to be sure that we can do it correctly. . . . I am scared to death that they are going to convince the president that they can do this overthrow of Saddam on the cheap, and we'll find ourselves in the middle of a swamp because we didn't plan to do it in the right way."[12]

Chuck Hagel, the Republican senator from Nebraska, also questioned the rationale for war, saying there was "absolutely no evidence" that Iraq possessed a nuclear capability. "You can take the country into a war pretty fast," Hagel said, "but you can't get out as quickly, and the public needs to know what the risks are."[13]

Before the war began, a number of individual analysts within the U.S. intelligence community questioned the White House case for war and complained that they were being pressured to stifle their misgivings. "Analysts at the working level in the intelligence community are feeling very strong pressure from the Pentagon to cook the intelligence books," said one official interviewed by the Knight Ridder news agency. Knight Ridder spoke to "a dozen other officials" who "echoed his views," although none would agree to speak publicly under their own names, for fear of retribution.[14]

The clash between the White House and career intelligence analysts was so strong that the Bush administration even created its own separate intelligence unit—the Policy Counterterrorism Evaluation Group, overseen by Douglas Feith, the Bush administration's undersecretary for defense. Since the 1990s, Feith had also been one of the vocal backers in Washington of Ahmed Chalabi's Iraqi National Congress, and he was a fierce ideological supporter of the administration's plans for war. According to General Tommy Franks, who led the invasion of Iraq, longtime military officials considered Feith "the fucking stupidest guy on the face of the earth," but he was praised by his mentor, Donald Rumsfeld. Secretary of State Colin Powell also had little use for the man, calling his operation a "Gestapo office" (although when push came to shove, both Franks and Powell ended up following Feith's lead).[15] In December 2002, investigative journalist Robert Dreyfuss reported that pressure from Feith and fellow travelers such as Deputy Defense Secretary Paul Wolfowitz was so strong that it was undermining morale within the CIA, "with career staffers feeling intimidated and pressured to justify the push for war."[16]

Five months before the start of war, *New York Times* reporters Eric Schmitt and Thom Shanker interviewed Paul Wolfowitz, who said that Feith's office was useful because "people who are pursuing a certain hypothesis will see certain facts that others won't, and not see other facts that others will. The lens through which you're looking for facts affects what you look for."[17] An anonymous defense official, also interviewed by Schmitt and Shanker, had a more cynical explanation. Feith's group, he said, was actually a vehicle for cherry-picking evidence and politicizing intelligence to fit the administration's view: "Wolfowitz and company disbelieve any analysis that doesn't support their own preconceived conclusions," the official said—an assessment that seems apt in light of the gap between the Bush administration's Feith-based assessments and the actual reality that Americans found once they occupied Iraq.

When they disagree with their boss, people who work for a government agency like the CIA are not terribly different from people who work for an HMO or an airline or a restaurant. They have bills to pay, career ambitions, concerns about their mortgage, children's college funds, alimony payments—all of the mundane reasons that motivate people to "go along to get along," even when they see something they don't like. Novelist Christopher Buckley has quipped that "I was only doing it to pay the bills" could be considered "the yuppie Nuremberg defense." In the case of Iraq, however, dissent from the White House party line was so strong that a number of career intelligence officials chose to resign rather than just follow orders:

➤ In September 2002, Greg Thielmann retired after twenty-five years in the State Department, the last four in the Bureau of Intelligence and Research. "The Al Qaeda connection and nuclear weapons issue were the only two ways that you could link Iraq to an imminent security threat to the U.S.," he said, "and the administration was grossly distorting the intelligence on both things."[18]

➤ Richard A. Clarke, the counterterrorism adviser on the U.S. National Security Council, resigned in January 2003 and wrote a book, *Against All Enemies*, which argues that the war in Iraq was a fatal diversion from the effort against terrorism.

➤ Rand Beers, a top White House counterterrorism adviser who had served under presidents Clinton and Reagan as well as both Bushes, quit five days before the start of war and volunteered to serve as a counterterrorism adviser to the presidential campaign of John Kerry. "The administration wasn't matching its deeds to its words in the war on terrorism. They're making us less secure, not more secure," he said.[19]

➤ Paul Pillar, the intelligence community's senior analyst for
the Middle East, stayed at his CIA job until 2005. After his
retirement, however, he wrote a devastating critique for *Foreign Affairs* magazine, stating that "official intelligence was
not relied on in making even the most significant national
security decisions, that intelligence was misused publicly to
justify decisions already made, that damaging ill will developed between [Bush] policymakers and intelligence officers, and that the intelligence community's own work was
politicized. . . . If the entire body of official intelligence
analysis on Iraq had a policy implication, it was to avoid
war—or, if war was going to be launched, to prepare for a
messy aftermath. . . . The administration used intelligence
not to inform decision-making, but to justify a decision already made. It went to war without requesting—and evidently without being influenced by—any strategic-level
intelligence assessments on any aspect of Iraq."[20]

In England, the office of Prime Minister Tony Blair committed itself publicly to echoing the White House line on Iraq, but
it, too, faced internal challenges from its own spy agency, MI6.
In March 2002, the Joint Intelligence Committee—the UK's
senior intelligence assessment body—issued an assessment of
Iraq's weapons capabilities that was considerably more modest
than Bush or Blair camps would claim publicly: "Intelligence
on Iraq's weapons of mass destruction (WMD) and ballistic missile programmes is sporadic and patchy. . . . From the evidence
available to us, we believe Iraq retains some production equipment, and some small stocks of [chemical weapons] agent pre-

cursors, and may have hidden small quantities of agents and weapons. . . . There is no intelligence on any [biological weapons] agent production facilities but one source indicates that Iraq may have developed mobile production facilities."[21]

Later that year, however, British intelligence assessments began to change—not because new evidence was coming to light but in deference to policy pressures from above. Evidence of those pressures appears in the "Downing Street Memo," a top-secret memorandum intended for viewing only by top British officials but leaked to the press in May 2005. It noted that Sir Richard Dearlove, the head of MI6, had "reported on his recent talks in Washington. There was a perceptible shift in attitude. Military action was now seen as inevitable. Bush wanted to remove Saddam, through military action, justified by the conjunction of terrorism and WMD. But the intelligence and facts were being fixed around the policy."[22]

Sometimes the "fixing" was embarrassingly amateurish. In February 2003, Blair's office circulated a dossier on Iraq that it claimed was an MI6 analysis but was embarrassed when forced to admit that the bulk of the dossier had actually been plagiarized from a paper written by a graduate student living in California. Dubbed the "dodgy dossier" by the British press, the document had actually been cobbled together at the last minute by junior aides to Alastair Campbell, Blair's press secretary. Further scrutiny found that other parts of the British dossier were lifted from *Jane's Intelligence Review*, part of the *Jane's* series of trade publications for soldiers and military contractors. Some of the plagiarized material had been written by analysts opposed to war with Iraq.[23]

The dossier was "obviously part of the Prime Minister's propaganda campaign," said Charles Heyman, editor of *Jane's World Armies*. "The intelligence services were not involved—I've had two people phoning me today to say, 'Look, we had nothing to do with it.' "[24]

There is a reason Tony Blair's spin doctors avoided using their own spy agency to produce the report. Actually, MI6 analysts disagreed with Blair's public position, and they made this clear by leaking an official British intelligence report to the BBC, which explicitly contradicted the government's public position by stating that there were no known links between Iraq and the Al Qaeda network.[25]

On March 17, 2003—two days before the start of the war with Iraq—former British foreign secretary Robin Cook resigned from Blair's cabinet in protest against the war. In his resignation speech to the British House of Commons, Cook expressly challenged the Bush and Blair governments' public assessment of Iraq as a military threat. "For four years as foreign secretary I was partly responsible for the western strategy of containment," Cook said. "Over the past decade that strategy destroyed more weapons than in the Gulf war, dismantled Iraq's nuclear weapons programme and halted Saddam's medium and long-range missiles programmes. Iraq's military strength is now less than half its size at the time of the last Gulf war. Ironically, it is only because Iraq's military forces are so weak that we can even contemplate its invasion. . . . We cannot base our military strategy on the assumption that Saddam is weak and at the same time justify pre-emptive action on the claim that he is a threat. Iraq probably has no weapons of mass destruction in the commonly understood sense of the term—namely a credible device capable of being delivered against a strategic city target."[26]

The Bush administration's current claim that "everybody else was wrong too" relies heavily on the failure of the U.S. news media to do a responsible job of reporting during the runup to war and the war itself. A study done in 2003 by Fairness and Accuracy in Reporting (FAIR) showed an overwhelming preponderance of pro-war viewpoints in television coverage of the war. It tabulated 1,617 on-camera sources that appeared in stories about Iraq according to their occupation, nationality, and position on the war and found that 64 percent of sources were pro-war, while antiwar voices were only 10 percent of sources. Among U.S. sources, only 3 percent were antiwar—this at a time when dissent was quite visible in U.S. society, with large antiwar demonstrations across the country and 27 percent of the public telling pollsters they opposed the war." Moreover, "Guests with anti-war viewpoints were almost universally allowed one-sentence soundbites taken from interviews conducted on the street. Not a single show in the study conducted a sit-down interview with a person identified as being against the war. Anti-war sources were treated so fleetingly that they often weren't even quoted by name. While 80 percent of all sources appearing on the nightly news shows are identified by name, 42 percent of anti-war voices went unnamed or were labeled with such vague terms as 'protester' or 'anti-war activist.' "[27]

Marianne Manilov, who worked as a communications consultant to U.S. peace groups, remembers that during the buildup to war period she tried to persuade U.S. news programs to feature guests who would offer a critical perspective. The guests that she offered included university scholars and other experts with impressive credentials. These guests were widely rejected. Instead, the antiwar voices that appeared in the media consisted of protesters at rallies and Hollywood celebrities such as Sean Penn, Susan Sarandon, or Janeane Garofalo. These programming choices delivered an implicit message that only scruffy radicals and Hollywood celebrities opposed the war.

Even so, it is instructive in retrospect to see what those voices said then and how well it stacks up against what everyone now knows to be the truth. Here, for example, is an excerpt from an interview that Tony Snow did with Janeane Garofalo on Fox News in February 2003, less than a month before the invasion began:

SNOW: Do you think [Saddam Hussein] is eager to obtain weapons of mass destruction?

GAROFALO: Yes, I think lots of people are eager to obtain weapons of mass destruction. But there's no evidence that he *has* weapons of mass destruction. There's been no evidence of him testing nuclear weapons. We have people that are in our face with nuclear weapons. We've got Iran and North Korea. We've got a problem with Pakistan. . . . There's a whole lot of people that are going nuclear. And I think that Saddam Hussein is actually, with the evidence, the least able to use nuclear weapons and the least obvious offender in that area at this moment. . . . But I also resent Rick—you know, Senator Santorum's assertions that this won't be particularly costly or lengthy. This is going to be economically devastating for us. And also, the assertion that inaction breeds terrorist strikes, that is ridiculous. Action in Iraq will make us decidedly less safe.[28]

How is it that Janeane Garofalo had a better analysis of Iraq's weapons programs—and of the likelihood of a protracted occupation—than the combined forces of the White House, U.S. intelligence agencies, and leading U.S. news media? Certainly it is not because she had more information than they did. Her superior analysis was based solely on her ability to think and reason independently, unfettered by the propaganda and group-think that has become the norm in government and elite media circles that shape and inform public policy.

"We Can't Leave Now, or the Terrorists Will Win"

The original rationale for war, of course, was that invading Iraq would get *rid* of terrorists. Instead, the occupation of Iraq provided a staging ground for what have now become daily terrorist attacks against U.S. soldiers and Iraqi civilians alike. Worse still, it has become a place where terrorists are developing skills and contacts that they will likely use to attack other targets in places such as Europe and the United States.

Remarkably, the Bush administration actually offered these attacks as signs of *progress* in the war on terror. "We are fighting them in Iraq so that we don't have to fight them at home," Bush declared—an argument that prompted some supporters of the war to begin describing Iraq as "carefully hung flypaper" where terrorists could be lured, trapped, and disposed of. Journalist Joshua Micah Marshall, however, offered a different metaphor, arguing that the "flypaper" theory should really be called the "dirty hospital" approach to fighting terror: "By creating a dirty hospital, we're going to create a place where we can fight the germs on our terms." [29] In reality, of course, creating a dirty hospital just provides a place where more germs can breed, and turning Iraq into a hotbed of terrorism has merely provided an opportunity for terrorists to meet, multiply, and practice their craft on live targets.

Consider, for example, the town of Salman Pak, south of Baghdad. In chapter four, we recounted some of the false information provided by the Iraqi National Congress that led the United States to believe that Iraq was training terrorists at a military facility near Salman Pak. A review of the evidence by the Senate Committee on Intelligence shows that the United States has subsequently acknowledged that those reports were unfounded, but thanks to the war, Salman Pak has since *become* a terrorist hotbed. By February 2005, the *Washington Post* reported, "Salman Pak is on the eastern edge of a region Iraqis have dubbed the 'triangle of death,' parts of which are so dangerous that many Iraqis are reluctant to travel its roads. Checkpoints manned by insurgents have sprung up along some of the region's highways as well as in such cities as Mahmudiyah and Latifiyah that have occasionally fallen under the sway of gunmen."[30] Sectarian conflicts between Shiite and Sunni Muslims turned the area into what Agence France-Presse called "Iraq's new hotspot where a motley army of Wahhabists, Saddamists and criminals are imposing their bloody rule. . . . Insurgents carry out almost daily car bomb and suicide attacks against the country's security forces." According to the head of Iraqi intelligence, Salman Pak had become "a guerrillas' fiefdom."[31] Later that year, U.S.-backed Shiite forces managed to take control of the town, using a combination of military force and interrogation techniques that included torture and beatings—further inflaming fear and resentment among the town's majority Sunni population and creating conditions in which more terrorist "germs" are likely to breed.[32]

This outcome is precisely what opponents of the war warned about from the start. In our 2003 book, *Weapons of Mass Deception*, we concluded by quoting the words of Egyptian president Hosni Mubarak, a U.S. ally. As the war commenced in March of that year, Mubarak predicted that "there will be 100 bin Ladens afterward."[33] So did Coleen Rowley, the FBI whistle-blower who was named *Time* magazine's 2002 "Person of the Year" after she exposed errors within the agency that might have allowed the 9/11 terrorists to carry out their plan. In a subsequent open letter to FBI director Robert Mueller, Rowley warned in March 2003 that invading Iraq would, "in all likelihood, bring an exponential increase in the terrorist threat to the U.S., both at home and abroad."[34] Lots of other people were making similar predictions back then, as even the conservative *National Review* admitted at the time (while also calling Rowley "a fool").[35]

Were these warnings correct? The available statistical evidence suggests that they were. Each year since 1985, the U.S. Department of State has been required to publish an annual report, titled *Patterns of Global Terrorism*, which tracks countries and groups involved in international terrorism. The 2004 edition of *Patterns of Global Terrorism* tallied attacks for 2003 (the first year of the war in Iraq). "You will find in these pages clear evidence that we are prevailing in the fight," declared Deputy Secretary of State Richard Armitage at the news conference announcing its release. Speaking at the same news conference, J. Cofer Black, the State Department coordinator for counterterrorism, said the report showed "a slight decrease" from the number of terrorist attacks that occurred the previous year.[36] That would be good news, of course—if it were true. In fact, the report was riddled with what State Department officials would later admit were administrative errors. As a result of those errors, the report undercounted by more than half the number of people killed and wounded—625 deaths instead of 307 as originally reported, and 3,646 people injured.[37] After correcting the mistakes, it turns out that 2003 saw 175 significant terrorist attacks (defined as attacks in which lives are lost or there is injury and property damage of more than ten thousand dollars)—the largest number of significant terrorist attacks since 1982.[38]

The following year, the numbers were even worse—651 significant terrorist attacks, nearly four times the number of the previous year's embarrassment, with 1,907 people killed and 9,300 wounded—roughly a tripling of the previous year's casualty toll.[39] Iraq alone saw 198 attacks that year—nearly the worldwide total for 2003—but even if all of those attacks were omitted, the number of terrorist attacks in the rest of the world were still more than double the all-time record. (So much for the "flypaper" theory.) The numbers were so bad that the Bush administration decided not to publish *Patterns of Global Terrorism* at all in 2005. In its place, the State Department created a new report, *Country Reports on Terrorism*, which omitted the statistical information provided in the previous reports. In a

State Department briefing, spokesman Richard Boucher said the numbers would be released someday, but "I don't know when."[40]

It should be noted, moreover, that the 651 terrorist attacks tallied for 2004 did not include attacks on U.S. *soldiers* in Afghanistan and Iraq, or even attacks on Iraqi civilians by other Iraqis. The long-standing U.S. definition of international terrorism, used by *Patterns of Global Terrorism*, defined it as violent acts against *noncombatants*, and it has to involve the territory or citizens of more than one country. (Timothy McVeigh's 1995 bombing of the federal building in Oklahoma City would also not fit this definition of terrorism.) The National Counterterrorism Center, a government agency created by President Bush in 2004, has compiled a separate report that does include other incidents not previously classed as terrorism (although attacks on soldiers are still excluded). Using this more inclusive definition, the number of terrorist incidents in 2004 would be 3,192.[41]

The National Counterterrorism Center's new database on terrorism was announced publicly in July 2005. That same month, a series of coordinated bombings hit London's subways and a bus during rush hour, killing 56 people and injuring 700—the deadliest single act of terrorism in the United Kingdom since the 1988 bombing of Pan Am Flight 103 over Lockerbie, Scotland. The terrorists, claiming affiliation with Al Qaeda, released a statement calling the London attack "revenge against the British Zionist crusader government in retaliation for the massacres Britain is committing in Iraq and Afghanistan." It was the second act of Al Qaeda violence against a European nation providing military support to the war in Iraq. The previous attack, a series of coordinated bombings against commuter trains in Madrid, killed 192 people and wounded 2,050 and triggered the electoral defeat of Spain's ruling party.

These events came as no surprise to Michael Scheuer, the former chief of the CIA's bin Laden unit until his resignation shortly after Bush's reelection in November 2004. Scheuer is the author of *Through Our Enemies' Eyes*, a biography of Osama bin Laden written in 2002. More recently, he is the author of *Imperial Hubris: Why the West Is Losing the War on Terror*, in which he bluntly criticizes the war on Iraq:

> There is nothing bin Laden could have hoped for more than the American invasion and occupation of Iraq. The U.S. invasion of Iraq is Osama bin Laden's gift from America, the one he has long and ardently desired, but never realistically expected. Think of it: Iraq is the second holiest land in Islam; a place where Islam had been long suppressed by Saddam; where the Sunni minority long dominated and brutalized the Shia majority; where order was kept only by the Baathist barbarity that prevented a long overdue civil war; and where, in the wake of Saddam's fall, the regional powers Iran and Saudi Arabia would intervene, at least clandestinely, to stop the creation of, respectively, a Sunni or Shia successor state. In short, Iraq without Saddam would obviously become what political scientists call a "failed state," a place bedeviled by its neighbors and—as in Afghanistan—a land where al Qaeda or al Qaeda–like organizations could thrive. Surely, thought bin

Laden, the Americans would not want to create this kind of situation. It would be, if you will, like deliberately shooting yourself in the foot. . . .

In the end, something much like Christmas had come for bin Laden, and the gift he received from Washington will haunt, hurt, and hound Americans for years to come.[42]

At a June 2005 Department of Defense briefing, not long after Vice President Dick Cheney declared that the insurgents in Iraq were "in their last throes," Lieutenant General James Conway noted that terrorist skills learned in Iraq were being transferred to Afghanistan, where it was "a little bit troubling" to see an increased use of improvised explosives devices (IEDs) due in part to "cross-pollination between the people in Iraq and Afghanistan."[43] Classified studies by the CIA and the State Department leaked to the press that same month. The studies showed that Iraq by then had become something it was not before the war began: "the prime training ground for foreign terrorists who could travel elsewhere across the globe and wreak havoc."[44] In fact, reported the *New York Times*, one classified CIA assessment said "Iraq may prove to be an even more effective training ground for Islamic extremists than Afghanistan was in Al Qaeda's early days, because it is serving as a real-world laboratory for urban combat. . . . [T]he urban nature of the war in Iraq was helping combatants learn how to carry out assassinations, kidnappings, car bombings and other kinds of attacks that were never a staple of the fighting in Afghanistan during the anti-Soviet campaigns of the 1980's."[45]

"If We Leave Now, All the Lives and Money We've Spent Will Have Been Wasted"

This argument, of course, begins by admitting that quite a bit of life and money has been lost already. It takes as its premise facts that contradict the earlier, rosy pronouncements of Bush administration officials and pro-war pundits such as Kenneth Adelman, a member of the Defense Policy Board and friend of Dick Cheney who predicted in February 2002 that "demolishing Hussein's military power and liberating Iraq would be a cakewalk."[46] Richard Perle predicted that the war "will be quicker and easier than many people think."[47]

Perhaps the most optimistic assessment came from Vice President Dick Cheney, in an interview with Tim Russert on NBC's *Meet the Press*. Russert asked about General Eric Shinseki's statement that several hundred thousand troops would need to remain in Iraq for several years to maintain stability. "I disagree," Cheney said, calling Shinseki's assessment "an overstatement."

"If your analysis is not correct," Russert said, "and we're not treated as liberators but as conquerors, and the Iraqis begin to resist, particularly in Baghdad, do you think the American people are prepared for a long, costly, and bloody battle with significant American casualties?"

"Well, I don't think it's likely to unfold that way, Tim," Cheney replied, "because I really do believe that we will be greeted as liberators."[48]

These predictions of a quick, easy war had consequences. Americans gambled on a losing bet, and they have had to pay for that gamble with treasure and with blood. To say now that those costs have been so high that we need to keep playing until we win is a classic gambler's fallacy and a weak argument by any measure. Just as a gambler has no guarantee that staying at the table will enable him to win back his losses, we have no reason to expect that remaining in Iraq will bring victory. To the contrary, the available evidence suggests that the longer we stay, the worse the ultimate reckoning will be.

Retired U.S. Army general William Odom is a Republican who formerly headed the National Security Agency under Ronald Reagan and also served as a deputy National Security Advisor. In April 2004—well ahead of John Murtha or other leading Democrats, who only began talking about troop withdrawal in late 2005—Odom argued that the United States needed to remove its forces "from that shattered country as rapidly as possible." The only issue yet to settle, he said, "is how high a price we're going to pay—less, by getting out sooner, or more, by getting out later."

Odom elaborated further in an interview with Katie Couric on the *Today* show. "But General Odom, as you well know, many people will say the United States simply cannot up and leave," Couric said. "What will it do for the reputation of this country around the world . . . if the administration doesn't have the stick-to-it-ness, if you will, to get the job done, to continue what was started in the first place?"

"We have already failed. Staying in longer makes us fail worse," Odom replied. "If we blindly say we should stick to it, we're misusing our power and we're making it worse. Let me put it more bluntly. Let's suppose you murdered somebody, and you suddenly look and say, 'We can't afford to have murdered this person, so therefore let's save him.' I think we've passed the chances to not fail. And now we are in a situation where we have to limit the damage. And the issue is just how much we are going to pay before we decide to limit the damage, not rescue ourselves by throwing good money after bad."[49]

At the time that Odom said those words, 725 American soldiers had died in Iraq. Since then, the toll has more than tripled.

CHAPTER SIX

Not Counting the Dead

Operation Desert Storm, the first U.S.-led war in the Persian Gulf, transformed American military strategy for managing public perceptions about the human costs of war. Leon Daniel, a veteran UPI war correspondent whose battlefield experience dates back to Vietnam, observed this firsthand when he visited the tip of the Neutral Zone between Saudi Arabia and Iraq on February 25, 1991, the day following the beginnings of the ground war. He was a member of the press pool assigned to cover the battle, but he and other reporters had not been allowed to witness the fighting itself, in which American soldiers attacked some eight thousand Iraqi defenders with tanks, artillery, howitzers, and rockets. By the time the press pool was allowed on the scene, the army was holding some two thousand Iraqi prisoners, but there were no bodies, no blood, no body parts, and no other visible signs of carnage. Daniel was puzzled by the lack of corpses, and it took months before he discovered how the dead had disappeared: They had been plowed under.

"Thousands of Iraqi soldiers, some of them alive and firing their weapons from World War I–style trenches, were buried by plows mounted on Abrams battle tanks," reported Patrick J. Sloyan, who interviewed soldiers involved in the operation. "The Abrams flanked the trench lines so that tons of sand from the plows funneled into the trenches. Just behind the tanks, actually straddling the trench line, came Bradleys pumping 7.62mm machine gun bullets into the Iraqi troops."[1]

"For all I know, we could have killed thousands. . . . What you saw was a bunch of buried trenches with people's arms and things sticking out of them," said army colonel Anthony Moreno, who commanded the lead brigade during the assault.[2] Colonel Lon Maggart, who commanded a separate brigade, estimated that his troops alone buried about 650 Iraqi soldiers. According to Sloyan, "One reason there was no trace of what happened in the Neutral Zone on those two days was that Armored Combat Earth Movers came behind the armored burial brigade, leveling the ground and smoothing away projecting Iraqi arms, legs and equipment." All told, some seventy miles of trenches and earthen bunkers were covered over during a two-day period.[3]

Peter Turnley, a photographer from Michigan, refused to participate in the army's pool system for journalists and was one of the few reporters to witness the "Mile of Death" before the bodies were cleared away. "When I arrived at the scene of this incredible carnage, strewn all over on this mile stretch were cars and trucks with wheels still turning, radios still playing, and there were bodies scattered along the road," he recalled. "Many people have asked the question 'how many people died' during the war with Iraq and the question has never been well answered. That first morning, I saw and photographed a U.S. Military 'graves detail' bury in large graves many bodies." Most of Turnley's photos, however, went unpublished and unseen by the public for more than a decade following the war.[4]

To this day, no one knows for sure how many Iraqis died during Operation Desert Storm. A 2003 analysis by Carl Conetta of the Project on Defense Alternatives (a defense policy analysis project) estimated that more than thirty-five hundred Iraqi civilians and probably more than twenty thousand soldiers were killed.[5] Other estimates have ranged from below ten thousand to more than one hundred thousand. The U.S.-led coalition and the regime of Saddam Hussein were enemies during the war, but they shared a common disinterest in recording or reporting the number of Iraqi casualties.

With regard to U.S. coalition forces, it was different matter. The number of dead was mercifully small: 293 U.S. dead, plus 65 Arab, British, and French. For those troops there was precise accounting of each casualty and cause of death. Their families were notified, funerals were held, honors were given. At the same time, military planners took pains to prevent the news media from broadcasting *images* of the dead. During the

U.S. invasion of Panama in December 1989, President George H. W. Bush had been embarrassed when he was seen on television joking at a White House conference at the same moment the first U.S. casualties were arriving at Dover Air Force Base. Three television networks broadcast live, split-screen images in which the president's lighthearted mood clashed with the somber images of flag-draped coffins.[6] In response, then defense secretary Dick Cheney imposed a ban on media coverage of returning U.S. casualties. The ban remained officially in place during Operation Desert Storm and continued under presidents Bill Clinton and George W. Bush, although in practice it was often ignored.

During the invasion of Iraq in 2003, American television in particular practiced a near-total blackout of disturbing images. The war even became humorous, as people mocked the clownish performances of Mohammed Saeed al-Sahaf, Iraq's information minister. Dubbed "Baghdad Bob" by Americans and "Comical Ali" by the British, al-Sahaf continued to insist that American troops were being "butchered" and "burnt" and committing suicide by the hundreds, even as American tanks were patrolling the streets only a few hundred meters from the location where one of his last press conferences was held. But while Baghdad Bob was engaged in propaganda that was inept and easy to ridicule, the American brand of spin was more sophisticated and effective. "There must have been two wars in Iraq. There was the war I saw and wrote about as a print journalist embedded with a tank company of the Army's 3rd Infantry Division (Mechanized). Then there was the war that many Americans saw, or wanted to see, on TV," wrote Ron Martz, a former marine and military-affairs reporter for the *Atlanta Journal-Constitution*. "I saw and wrote about a war that was confusing and chaotic, as are all wars. It was a war in which plans and missions changed almost daily—and on one occasion changed three times in an hour. It was a war in which civilians died and were horribly wounded. . . . The war they saw, or thought they saw, on TV was meticulously planned, flawlessly executed—and not a single member of the armed forces had a complaint or problem. Few civilians died in that war."[7] Martz described receiving angry e-mail from newspaper readers who complained that his reports from the battlefield did not match up with what they were seeing on television:

> When I wrote in one story about "bloody street fighting in Baghdad," it appeared the morning TV viewers were seeing jubilant Marines and Iraqi civilians tearing down statues of Saddam Hussein on the eastern side of the Tigris River. Some readers, believing all of Baghdad was like that, were livid. They did not grasp the fact that, on the western side of the river, pitched battles were still taking place. Because they did not see it on TV, it was not happening. And it did not fit their view of the war. . . .
>
> One woman even suggested I start watching more Fox TV to get an unbiased view of the war. I resisted the urge to tell her that the TV reception was miserable in the back of the armored personnel carrier in which I was riding.
>
> The criticism was not limited to me. They even criticized soldiers for doing what all soldiers do—complain. When I voiced complaints from soldiers about lack of mail, water,

and spare parts, they were called "whiners" and "crybabies." And when I quoted one soldier who had been under fire almost daily for four weeks complaining about faulty intelligence, one reader suggested he be stripped of his uniform and sent home in disgrace.

A friend recently told me she believes TV has significantly "dumbed down" the American public and lowered the collective IQ. After seeing and hearing the public reaction to this war, I am beginning to believe she is right.[8]

Even so, the low number of coalition casualties by the time Baghdad fell made it possible to imagine that the war in Iraq would be a relatively blood-free affair. As in Operation Desert Storm and the invasion of Afghanistan, the operation used a combination of devastating aerial attacks combined with overwhelming technological superiority in ground operations to crush their Iraqi opponents. The march to Baghdad was so rapid that the main problem encountered by troops was the difficulty maintaining adequate deliveries of food and fuel at the front of the line. By the time President Bush declared an "end to major combat operations in Iraq" on May 1, 2003, only 173 coalition troops had died—140 Americans and 33 British.[9] Bush also used the occasion to praise the modern technology of war, which he said had helped protect Iraq's civilian population: "For hundreds of years of war, culminating in the nuclear age, military technology was designed and deployed to inflict casualties on an ever-growing scale. . . . Today, we have the greater power to free a nation by breaking a dangerous and aggressive regime. With new tactics and precision weapons, we can achieve military objectives without directing violence against civilians. No device of man can remove the tragedy from war; yet it is a great moral advance when the guilty have far more to fear from war than the innocent."[10]

The government was not merely determined to minimize the *number* of dead. It also worked to minimize *reporting* on the deaths that did occur. On the eve of war in March 2003, the Pentagon sent a directive to U.S. military bases. "There will be no arrival ceremonies for, or media coverage of, deceased military personnel returning to or departing from Ramstein [Germany] airbase or Dover [Delaware] base, to include interim stops," it stated.[11] And whereas previous presidents including Ronald Reagan, George H.W. Bush, Jimmy Carter, and Bill Clinton personally attended memorials and funerals for soldiers killed in action during their presidencies, President Bush refrained from participation in funerals.[12]

In the summer of 2003, the euphoria of victory began to fade as a steady trickle of new casualties in Iraq demonstrated that the invasion of Iraq was only a prelude to the real war of occupation. By July 17, the Pentagon reported another thirty-three combat deaths since the "end of major combat." As Greg Mitchell noted in *Editor and Publisher* magazine, that number was actually rather misleading. If noncombat casualties were included, the actual number would have been eighty-five. The "non-hostile" causes of death included helicopter crashes, illness, drowning, heatstroke, accidental firearm discharge, suicide, and vehicle accidents. "Even if killed in a non-hostile action, these soldiers are no less dead, their families no less aggrieved," Mitchell observed. "Nevertheless, the media continues to report the much lower figure of 33 as if those are the only deaths that count."[13]

Cher Shocked

One of the first public voices to talk about U.S. casualties with any passion was Cher, the singer and movie actress. Following a morale visit to wounded soldiers at Walter Reed Hospital, Cher telephoned the call-in line at C-SPAN: "I had the occasion the other day to spend the entire day with troops that had come back from Iraq and had been wounded," she said before describing her experiences with young men who had lost arms and legs in the war. "They had the most unbelievable courage," she said. "It took everything that I have as a person to—to not, you know, break down while I was talking to these guys. . . . And also I wonder why are none of Cheney, Wolfowitz, Bremer, the president—why aren't they taking pictures with all these guys? Because I don't understand why these guys are so hidden and why there aren't pictures of them, because you know, talking about the dead and the wounded, that's two different things, but these wounded are so devastatingly wounded. It's unbelievable. It's just unbelievable to me. You know, if you're going to send these people to war, then don't hide them. Have some news coverage where people are sitting and talking to these guys and seeing how they are and seeing their spirit. It's just—I think it's a crime."[14]

The pop star's instincts were right. Wounded soldiers were

less likely to die in Iraq than in previous wars, but this was a mixed blessing. Compared to World War II, when one out of three injuries resulted in death, fewer than one in eight injuries in Iraq was fatal, thanks to better helmets and body armor combined with advances in medical technology. Unfortunately, this also meant that many of the survivors suffered from more serious, long-term injuries than in past wars, including burns, amputations, and damaged spinal cords. The use of improvised explosive devices by insurgents also contributed to a high number of brain injuries. "So many who survive explosions—more than half—sustain head injuries that doctors say anyone exposed to a blast should be checked for neurological problems," reported the *New York Times*. Dr. Thomas E. Bowen, who was a surgeon in Vietnam before heading a veterans' hospital in Florida, noticed the difference: "In Vietnam, they'd bring in a soldier with two legs blown off by a mine, but he wouldn't have the head injuries. Some of the patients we have here now, they can't swallow, they can't talk, they're paralyzed and blind."[15]

By September 2003, nearly ten soldiers per day were being officially declared "wounded in action," but U.S. Central Command only released the number of wounded when asked, and reporters almost never did. One of the exceptions was Vernon Lobe of the *Washington Post*. "With no fanfare and almost no public notice, giant C-17 transport jets arrive virtually every night at Andrews Air Force Base outside Washington on medical evacuation missions. Since the war began, more than 6,000 service members have been flown back to the United States," he reported on September 2, four months after Bush declared the "end to major combat." That number included "1,124 wounded in action, 301 who received non-hostile injuries in vehicle accidents and other mishaps, and thousands who became physically or mentally ill."[16]

Even the Disabled American Veterans (DAV), a long-standing support organization for returning soldiers, came up against new policies restricting its access to wounded veterans in Walter Reed Army Hospital and Bethesda Naval Hospital. Citing the Patriot Act and privacy concerns, the Department of Defense refused to allow DAV representatives to talk with wounded veterans unless the veterans specifically asked for them. "Even then an escort from the hospital staff accompanies our [National Service Officer], thus negating the confidentiality of the session with the combat injured veteran," complained Frank D. Williams, the DAV's Ohio state commander.[17] Another DAV official, Tom Keller, put the matter more bluntly: "I have my own feelings about why the Bush administration is bringing the casualties back to the States in the middle of the night and wants to keep organizations like the DAV away from them. I believe the administration wants to keep the American people in the dark about the number of troops being wounded, the severity of the injuries they are receiving and the types of illnesses that may be surfacing."[18]

DAV executive director Dave Gorman—who lost both of his legs in Vietnam—made his complaint in the form of a letter to Secretary of Defense Donald Rumsfeld. "For more than six decades the DAV has always been granted access to military hospitals so our professionally-trained and fully-accredited representatives could provide such crucial information and counseling to service members to help smooth their transition from military to civilian life," he wrote. "Sadly, that is no longer the case. The current policies of the Department of Defense citing the Privacy Act and security are preventing our skilled representatives from carrying out our congressionally-chartered mission. . . . The American public would be outraged if these restrictions became public knowledge."[19]

The Beat Goes On

U.S. publications periodically updated the death toll for U.S. soldiers, and local newspapers reported on individual deaths as they occurred. In the spring of 2003, CNN and the *Washington Post* launched special sections on their websites that provided photographs and names of U.S. and coalition casualties.[20] A similar memorial was begun in December 2003 by the *Army Times*, a civilian newspaper that is sold mainly on military bases. It used eight pages of its year-end review to run photos of the more than five hundred soldiers who had died by then in Iraq and Afghanistan.[21] According to the paper's managing editor, Robert Hodierne, getting the photos was a struggle because "The military doesn't give out so many photos of the dead."

In April 2004, a month that saw the deaths of 140 soldiers, Americans finally saw their first image of flag-draped coffins returning from Iraq. The photo was not taken by a journalist, however. It was taken by Tami Silicio of Seattle, who worked with her husband for Maytag Aircraft, a private company that handled cargo shipments for the U.S. military. On April 7, the cargo consisted of coffins being loaded for their journey back to the States. Using her digital camera, Silicio took photos of the scene and e-mailed them to a friend back home with a note that said, "Last night at work we sent home 22." Moved by the power of the image, her friend took the photo to the *Seattle Times*, which asked for permission to print the photo in their April 18 edition, under the headline "The Somber Task of Honoring the Fallen."[22] "I didn't have any aspirations of sending my picture to the paper, but I agreed to publish it because I felt that if families knew how well their loved ones were being treated on the way home, it would help comfort them in a time when nothing else can," Silicio said.[23] Its publication, however, brought retaliation. Under pressure from the Pentagon, Silicio's employer fired her along with her husband, although her photo prompted an outpouring of supportive letters and phone calls from *Seattle Times* readers.[24]

Silicio's photo also set off a chain of events that helped raise the profile of antiwar sentiments in the United States. Although some people criticized the decision to publish the photo, several parents of fallen soldiers told reporters that they wanted newspapers to publish photos documenting their pain and sacrifice. One of those was Bill Mitchell, whose son Michael had died in Sadr City on April 4. "I am quite positive that he was inside one of those coffins in the picture," Mitchell wrote in a letter to *Seattle Times* reporter Hal Bernton. "I am happy that you ran the story and showed the picture. I would like everyone to know the devastation that this event has brought upon Mike's family and friends. In fact, Mike's grandpa at 86 says that this is the worst thing that has happened in his entire life—that says a lot right

there! . . . Things are getting worse in Iraq and if there is anything that I can do so that other parents can be spared the pain
that is happening in my life, I will do it. In fact, I would be willing to furnish you a picture of my son in his casket if you would
like to run it in your paper. Sort of a follow-up story that would
just take it one step further than the picture shown inside the airplane with a bunch of anonymous flag-draped coffins. I don't
think I can be fired, as I do not have a job! I am currently in Germany taking care of my son's fiancee because officially, she is
not recognized by the U.S. Army even though she was the reason that he reenlisted twice; the last time being just 3 weeks
prior to his death."[25]

He also sent a copy of his letter to Greg Mitchell (no relation)
at *Editor and Publisher*, the newspaper industry trade publication. The letter prompted Greg Mitchell to pen an editorial titled "When Will the First Major Newspaper Call for a Pullout
in Iraq?" It noted that the vast majority of American newspapers
favored staying the course in Iraq, even as retired U.S. Army
lieutenant general William Odom, director of the National Security Agency during the Reagan administration, advocated a
phased U.S. pullout. "And yet no major newspaper has explored
this idea," Mitchell wrote. "Are you ready, now, to think the un-
thinkable? Who will be the first in line to call for a phased withdrawal, not more troops?"[26] Six days later he got his answer, as
USA Today founder Al Neuharth penned an editorial which
stated, "Only a carefully planned withdrawal can clean up the
biggest military mess miscreated in the Oval Office and miscar-
ried by the Pentagon in my 80-year lifetime."[27]

The publicity also helped bring Bill Mitchell together with

another grieving parent—Cindy Sheehan, whose son Casey was killed in Sadr City on the same day as Mike Mitchell and whose body was on the same flight. The two soldiers had not known each other in life, but their deaths brought their parents together. A year later, Sheehan led a growing protest vigil outside Bush's ranch in Crawford, Texas, and Bill Mitchell flew in from California to stand by her side.[28]

The Memory Hole

As it turns out, the same government that objected to Tami Silicio's photograph was shooting hundreds of pictures of soldiers' caskets and quietly filing them away. The government photos were uncovered, not by the traditional news media but by a website run by a single individual—Russ Kick's TheMemoryHole .org, which archives government files, corporate memos, court documents, and other "material that is in danger of being lost, is hard to find, or is not widely known." After Kick learned of the government ban on distributing photos of caskets, he filed a request under the U.S. Freedom of Information Act in November 2003, asking for "All photographs showing caskets (or other devices) containing the remains of US military personnel at Dover AFB. This would include, but not be limited to, caskets arriving, caskets departing, and any funerary rites/rituals being performed." His request was rejected, but he appealed the ruling and won. On April 14, 2004, the air force sent him a CD containing 361 digital photographs, which he promptly added to his website. The incident, according to former Minneapolis newspaper reporter Steve Yelvington, "demonstrates that freedom of the press belongs to the people, not just to corporations, and that sunshine laws are for all of us, not just for the press."[29] A second lawsuit under the Freedom of Information Act, filed by journalism professor Ralph Begleiter, forced the Pentagon to release several hundred additional images a year later.[30]

On April 30, 2004, the controversy over mentioning the dead spilled onto television, when Ted Koppel's *Nightline* program on ABC ran a program titled "The Fallen," which consisted of Koppel simply reading the names of the 721 U.S. soldiers who had died by then in Iraq, as their faces flashed briefly on the screen. The show was not aired, however, on ABC affiliates owned by the Sinclair Broadcast Group, a media company which is the single largest operator of local television stations in the United States. Sinclair, which is known for its conservative political leanings, barred its ABC-affiliated stations from showing the program and issued a statement saying that the show "appears to be motivated by a political agenda designed to undermine the efforts of the United States in Iraq."[31] (Later that year, Sinclair would become a topic of another controversy, when it announced plans to broadcast a sharply critical documentary about U.S. presidential candidate John Kerry less than a week before election day.)

Actually, the images of flag-draped coffins and still photos of the faces of the dead were exercises in minimalism compared to the photos that have been published from previous wars. During the U.S. Civil War, Matthew Brady's photographs of bodies sprawled across the battlefield at Antietam were incomparably more graphic and shocking to the viewers who saw them. "Let him who wishes to know what war is look at this series of illustrations," commented Oliver Wendell Holmes, Sr. (the father of the future U.S. Supreme Court justice) after viewing Brady's exhibition: "These wrecks of manhood thrown together in careless heaps or ranged in ghastly rows for burial were alive but yesterday. . . . Many, having seen it and dreamed of its horrors, would lock it up . . . that it might not thrill or revolt those whose souls sickens at such sights. It was so nearly like visiting the battlefield to look over these views, that all the emotions excited by the actual sight of the stained and sordid scene, strewed with rags and wrecks, came back to us, and we buried them in the recesses of our cabinet as we would have buried the mutilated remains of the dead they too vividly represented. . . . [It] gives us . . . some conception of what a repulsive, brutal, sickening, hideous thing it is, this dashing together of two frantic mobs to which we give the name of armies."[32] During World War II, *Life* magazine featured a photo of a soldier's burial on the cover of its July 5, 1943, edition, and President Roosevelt actually encouraged media coverage of harsh conditions on the battlefield, in the belief that an understanding of soldiers' suffering would steel Americans to endure hardships at home.[33]

The Tomb of the Unknown Civilian

There is a difference between the importance Americans accorde their own casualties and the way they think about others, and that difference was reflected in the media coverage. Government officials made an effort to minimize publicity about

American casualties that they thought would be demoralizing, but the deaths nevertheless were tallied. On any given day, it was possible to find an exact number. Websites such as the Iraq Coalition Casualty Count (www.icasualties.org) or Paul DeRooij's "Data Sheet of US-UK Military Fatalities" provided monthly charts and breakout statistics by ethnicity and age. As the death toll crept upward, U.S. news media recorded the grim benchmarks: 1,000 soldiers dead by September 2004; 2,000 in October 2005.

These benchmarks would have come sooner if they had used statistics based on all soldier deaths, but the deaths of non-Americans were considered less newsworthy. On October 25, the date that marked 2,000 U.S. deaths, few reporters bothered to mention, even in passing, that 199 soldiers from other countries had also been killed (half of them British) — not to mention 3,500 deaths of U.S.-trained Iraqi police and military. The *Washington Post* reported on the 2,000 milestone with poignant reporting on Americans who were coping with the loss of loved ones, but made no mention at all of the deaths of foreign soldiers. Its only mention of Iraqi deaths came in a single paragraph near the bottom of the story. "Based on fragmented reports," it stated, "the number of enemy Iraqi fighters killed appears to be several times greater than the U.S. fatalities, while independent estimates of the number of dead Iraqi civilians range from 20,000 to 30,000."[34] But these numbers almost certainly understated Iraqi losses.

While U.S. casualties were recorded with precision, the number of Iraqi casualties, both civilian and military, remained elusive. During the earlier invasion of Afghanistan,

General Tommy R. Franks, the commander of U.S. forces, had declared that "we don't do body counts."[35] The military's attitude during Operation Iraqi Freedom was similar. No specific numbers were offered in briefings or public reports, although officials used vague adjectives to characterize the numbers. "The loss of innocent life is a tragedy for anyone involved in it, but the numbers are really very low," said Paul Bremer, the head of the Provisional Coalition Authority in August 2003.[36] But just a few days earlier, Colonel Guy Shields, another U.S. military spokeman, had said that the U.S. didn't *have* any numbers. It was not trying to count civilian deaths, he said, because doing so was just too difficult: "Well, we do not keep records for the simple reason that there is no really accurate way," Shields said at a press briefing on August 4. "In terms of statistics we have no definite estimates of civilian casualties for the whole campaign. It would be irresponsible to give firm estimates given the wide range of variables. For example we've had cases where during a conflict, we believed civilians had been wounded and perhaps killed, but by the time our forces have a chance to fully assess the outcomes of a contact, the wounded or the dead civilians have been removed from the scene. Factors such as this make it impossible for us to maintain an accurate account."[37]

It ought to be obvious upon even a moment's reflection that this argument is nonsense. Even if it is impossible to obtain a perfect casualty count, it is still possible to make meaningful estimates. Casualty statistics exist for the Crusades, the Hundred Years' War in Europe, the English Civil Wars, the First and

Second World Wars, the Russian Revolution of 1917, the Nationalist-Communist Civil War in China, the Korean War, Vietnam, and the Russian war in Afghanistan—to name just a few. Compared to the war in Iraq, those wars all occurred under conditions that were less conducive to recordkeeping, and with weaker technological capabilities for battlefield monitoring. If statistics do not exist for Iraq, it is not for lack of ability to compile them; it is because of an unwillingness to do so.

In the post-9/11 political environment in the United States, it was not just the government that chose this course. For journalists and many members of the general public as well, the wars in Afghanistan and Iraq were acts of retaliation, and they simply did not want to be bothered by hearing how many innocent people might suffer as a result. During the war in Afghanistan, the *News Herald* in Panama City, Florida, sent a memo to its editorial staff. "DO NOT USE photos on Page 1A showing civilian casualties from the U.S. war on Afghanistan," it warned. "Our sister paper in Fort Walton Beach has done so and received hundreds and hundreds of threatening e-mails and the like. . . . DO NOT USE wire stories which lead with civilian casualties from the U.S. war on Afghanistan. They should be mentioned further down in the story. If the story needs rewriting to play down the civilian casualties, DO IT. The only exception is if the U.S. hits an orphanage, school or similar facility and kills scores or hundreds of children. . . . Failure to follow any of these or other standing rules could put your job in jeopardy."[38]

As we documented in *Weapons of Mass Deception*, pressure to present the war in a favorable light produced very different coverage of the war in the United States than in Europe or other parts of the world. During the invasion phase, European and Australian publications were ten times as likely to mention the U.S. use of cluster bombs—antipersonnel devices that cause a large number of civilian casualties. (According to a study by Human Rights Watch, "Most of the civilian casualties attributable to Coalition conduct in the ground war appear to have been the result of ground-launched cluster munitions."[39] And even when cluster bombs *were* mentioned in the American press, many of the reports focused on denials by U.S. officials that they were being used (denials that have subsequently been proven false), or on efforts to protect U.S. soldiers from their effects.[40]

In Afghanistan and Iraq alike, the closest thing to systematic efforts at counting the dead came not from journalists or the government but from motivated private individuals. During the war in Afghanistan, University of New Hampshire economics professor Marc Herold, a critic of the war, attempted to compile a count of Afghani deaths by tallying the numbers in verified reports from aid agencies, eyewitnesses, and the world's media. Herold's methodology ignored soldiers and looked only at civilian deaths, and since some deaths in wartime never get publicly reported, undoubtedly he missed some of the casualties that were actually occurring. He made no attempt to tally indirect deaths caused by land mines, lack of water, food, or medicine. His initial report also included some errors, reflecting inaccuracies and inconsistencies in some of the underlying news reports, as well as double counting due to confused place names in some of the reports that Herold cited. After adjusting as best he could for those factors, by the end of July 2002, Herold had arrived at a stable estimate of between 3,000 and 3,400 Afghan civilians killed since the start of war on October 7.[41] His effort to tally the dead came under instant attack from supporters of the war such as popular conservative blogger Glenn Reynolds, who called him a "polypseudomathicator."[42] Other conservative bloggers called him an "anti-war propagandist," a "charlatan," "pseudo-scholar," "the professor who can't count straight," "full of shit," and an "eternal liar."[43]

With the commencement of war in Iraq, Herold served as adviser to a British-based team of researchers and antiwar activists who established the Iraq Body Count project (IraqBodyCount.net), an Internet-based dossier of Iraqi civilian casualties that was compiled using a methodology similar to Herold's, with additional care taken to cross-check and review results. They also required two independent agencies to publish a report before adding it to their count. Where different news stories reported a different civilian death toll from a single incident, they added the low number to their "minimum" estimate and the high number to their "maximum" estimate. Even so, their requirement that deaths had to be first reported in the news as a condition for being counted virtually guaranteed that even their "maximum" estimate was an undercount. "We are not a news organization ourselves and like everyone else can only base our information on what has been reported so far," they stated. "What we are attempting to provide is a credible compilation of civilian deaths that have been reported by recognized sources. . . . It is likely that many if not most civilian casualties will go unreported by the media. That is the sad nature of war."[44]

In July 2005, Iraq Body Count issued a news release on the

number of civilian casualties in the first two years of war. It had tallied 24,865 civilian deaths during that period.[45] Its conclusions were reported prominently in leading newspapers throughout Latin America: Argentina's *La Nación*, Mexico's *Reforma*, Brazil's *Folha de São Paolo*. "Similarly, virtually all British dailies carried the story in full on July 20," noted *Miami Herald* columnist Andres Oppenheimer. "But in the U.S. press, the Iraq Body Count report got short shrift. From a search in the NexisLexis database, the *New York Times* and the *Los Angeles Times* were among the few to carry staff-written stories on the report. The *Washington Post* mentioned it in passing, in the last paragraph of a story on the Iraq war, accompanied by a chart on civilian casualties. Most other U.S. newspapers, including the *Chicago Tribune*, the *Houston Chronicle*, the *Atlanta Journal-Constitution* and *The Herald* didn't carry the story in their print editions."[46] The conservative *National Review* responded to the report by denouncing Iraq Body Count as a "hard-left antiwar group."[47]

Another, less systematic effort at counting the dead was mounted by Marla Ruzicka, a peace activist from California who, like Herold, got her start counting casualties in Afghanistan. Unlike Herold, Ruzicka didn't rely on news reports. She did her research in person, going door to door with the assistance of interpreters. By herself, of course, she wasn't able to cover an entire country. Rather than compiling a complete count, her goal was to obtain financial compensation and assistance for some of the surviving family members of people who had been killed. A young, attractive blonde, Ruzicka managed to charm U.S. soldiers and diplomats as well as the Iraqi families she was trying to help. In 2005, however, she herself became a casualty of the war when she was killed by a suicide bomber while traveling with a U.S. military convoy.[48] Her death brought effusions of grief and praise for her work from people who knew her such as Chris Albritton, a freelance war correspondent working for *Time* magazine and other publications.[49] *FrontPage Magazine*, a popular conservative online magazine, responded to her death with an orgy of vindictive slander, calling her death "poetic justice" and describing her as an "activist bimbette" whose "sole purpose is to legitimize our enemies, cause problems for U.S. troops already in harm's way, and morally equate dead terrorists with victims of 9/11."[50]

The methods used by the Iraq Body Count and Marla Ruzicka were not intended to provide a comprehensive estimate of the total number of Iraqi deaths. To date, the best available estimate remains a study that was conducted in 2004 for a team of medical researchers from Johns Hopkins University, Columbia University, and Baghdad's Al-Mustansiriya University and published in the *Lancet*, England's leading medical journal.[51] The *Lancet* researchers, led by John Hopkins epidemiologist Les F. Roberts, were familiar with the techniques used to study disease and mortality. Roberts had studied mortality caused by war since 1992, leading surveys in locations including Bosnia, Congo, and Rwanda. His Congo research had been treated as front-page news by the *New York Times* and had been quoted in public testimony by public figures including Colin Powell and Tony Blair.

Roberts's team in Iraq used a method similar to those he had used elsewhere. It did not attempt to distinguish between civilian and military deaths, and it looked at all causes of death—not just military violence but also crime, chaos, lack of sanitation and medical care. Rather than simply count deaths, its goal was to estimate the number of *excess* deaths and the *causes* of death. If supporters of the war were genuinely concerned about the welfare of Iraqis, this is precisely the type of information that ought to interest them. And it was possible, in theory at least, that a complete mortality study would actually show that the invasion was saving or would save lives, by eliminating the malnutrition, poverty, and government violence that existed under Saddam Hussein. During the runup to war, some of its supporters actually claimed that this would happen. "The only reason to fight this war is that doing so will save lives," said Marvin Olasky, a conservative thinker and occasional adviser of President Bush. (It was Olasky who coined the term "compassionate conservatism.") Olasky recognized that war would inevitably kill some civilians: "Even though our intent is only to take out Saddam Hussein and his soldiers, it is certain that some innocent people will suffer alongside the guilty." Nevertheless, he added, "my sense is that President Bush's policy is the one most likely to minimize the loss of innocent life."[52] If this were indeed the case, the *Lancet* study would have provided evidence of it. And a complete mortality study has other, more immediately practical benefits. Knowing the most common causes of death can help in directing assistance and compensation efforts for the victims, and it can also help planners design military and reconstruction strategy with an eye to reducing future deaths. Counting the dead is not just an exercise in morbid curiosity. It is important for humanitarian reasons.

For a benchmark, the *Lancet* team sought to determine the death rate in Iraq before the U.S. invasion and compare it against the death rate afterward. Their methodology was similar to the "cluster sample survey" technique commonly used for studying health and mortality in developing countries. They mapped Iraq according to its population density and used a random number generator to select points on the map, sampled so that "every household in Iraq had an equal chance that we would visit them," as Roberts explained in an interview.[53] "We randomly allocated 33 points which we would go visit, and we went out to the villages or towns and picked up that point, and visited the 30 houses closest," he said. "We've got 33 neighborhoods. We visited 30 houses in each one. And we asked people: Who lives here now? Who lived here the first of January, 2002? Had anyone been born? Had anyone died? And at the end of the interview, if they had reported someone dead, on a sub-sample, we asked, can you show us the death certificate? And about 82% of the time, they could do that."[54]

Merely conducting the study was risky for the researchers. Roberts initially planned to visit Iraq in the spring of 2004, but his trip had to be postponed out of concern for his own safety following the beheading by terrorists of American businessman Nick Berg. He finally made the trip in September to train the six Iraqi field researchers—five of them doctors—who would be going door-to-door to conduct the survey.[55] Given the country's level of overall violence, going door-to-door was too dangerous for an American, and it was dangerous even for Iraqis. It was especially dangerous in Fallujah, which happened to contain one of the thirty-three randomly selected interview sites—so dangerous that only one of the Iraqi researchers was willing to travel there. Following the killing and mutilation of U.S. military contractors there in March, U.S. Marines had placed Fallujah under siege in an anti-insurgent campaign called Operation Vigilant Resolve, followed by air strikes and other attacks in preparation for Operation Phantom Fury, a concentrated assault on the city that would begin in November. Not surprisingly, these circumstances also meant that the death toll recorded by the interviewer in Fallujah was dramatically higher than in the other points visited for the study. It was so off the charts compared to the other points in their sample that the researchers decided to classify it as an anomaly and excluded it from their statistical analysis.

Even after excluding Fallujah, the results were chilling. Before the invasion, the major causes of death for Iraqis were heart attacks, strokes, and other chronic disorders. Afterward, the *Lancet* reported, "violence was the primary cause of death. Violent deaths were widespread, reported in 15 of 33 clusters, and were mainly attributed to coalition forces. Most individuals reportedly killed by coalition forces were women and children. The risk of death from violence in the period after the invasion was 58 times higher . . . than in the period before the war. . . . Making conservative assumptions, we think that about 100,000 excess deaths, or more, have happened since the 2003 invasion of Iraq. Violence accounted for most of the excess deaths and air strikes from coalition forces accounted for most violent deaths."[56]

As with any study that relies on statistical sampling, this one had a margin of error. The *Lancet* researchers had compiled information on 7,438 people preinvasion and 7,868 people postinvasion. Extrapolating from this sampling, they used statistical methods to estimate the number of deaths in Iraq's entire population of twenty-five million people. When this sort of extrapolation is done, the standard scientific procedure is to report the result as a minimum and maximum value—a "confidence interval" derived from statistical analysis which finds a 95 percent probability that the two limiting values enclose the true number. The *Lancet* researchers calculated a 95 percent confidence interval of between 8,000 to 194,000 excess deaths. This is quite a wide interval, and what it means is that the *Lancet* study was not very precise—an inevitability, perhaps, given that it was conducted with a budget of only $40,000. A better funded study that samples a larger subset of the Iraqi population would improve its precision. The fact that the *Lancet* study was imprecise does not mean, however, that it was meaningless or that the true number is equally likely to fall anywhere within that interval. Probabilities cluster like a bell curve around the center, which in this case was 98,000. Merely using a 90 rather than a 95 percent confidence interval would have produced a lower bound of 40,000 rather than 8,000. Moreover, the fact that the researchers excluded their Fallujah data from analysis made it more likely that they were underestimating rather than overestimating the true death toll.

For Les Roberts, one of the most shocking things about the

study was the discovery that violence had been the primary cause of death since the invasion. In most of the other wars he had studied, malnutrition and disease were the primary killers. Once the data analysis was completed, he wanted to "get this information out before the U.S. election" in the hope that it would encourage political candidates from both parties to commit publicly to policies aimed at minimizing Iraqi deaths. He submitted the paper to *Lancet* editor Richard Horton, who agreed. The study was released publicly on October 29—the Friday before the U.S. presidential election. An accompanying editorial by Horton stated that the study by Roberts and company "has been extensively peer-reviewed, revised, edited, and fast-tracked to publication because of its importance to the evolving security situation in Iraq."[57]

The *Lancet* study was widely praised by public health researchers and received front-page play in newspapers throughout Europe but was virtually ignored in the U.S. news media. It was not mentioned at all on the Fox, ABC, and CBS networks. NBC mentioned it in a report that lasted twenty-one seconds. On National Public Radio, *Morning Edition* and *All Things Considered* devoted forty-five seconds to it.[58] The *Los Angeles Times* and the *Chicago Tribune* gave it about four hundred words of mention apiece in stories buried on their inside pages.[59] The *New York Times* gave it 770 words, also on an inside page. It stated that the study "is certain to generate intense controversy," but the *Times* has published nothing further on it since.[60] The *Washington Post* also buried the story on an inside page and quoted Marc E. Garlasco, a senior military analyst at Human Rights Watch, as saying, "These numbers seem to be inflated." (The *Post* also inaccurately described the 100,000 figure as an estimate of "civilian casualties," when in fact the study did not distinguish between civilian and military deaths.)[61]

In fact, Garlasco had not read the *Lancet* paper at the time he was interviewed by the *Post*, and he now regrets his remark. When the reporter phoned, he says, his initial response was, "I haven't read it. I haven't seen it. I don't know anything about it, so I shouldn't comment on it. . . . Like any good journalist, he got me to."[62] Garlasco has subsequently studied the *Lancet* report and is impressed by it. "First of all, I'm not a statistician. I know absolutely nothing about it, and when I then went and spoke to statisticians, they said, 'Oh no, you know, the method that he's using is a really accurate one. This is something that we use in studies all throughout the world, and it's a generally accepted model.' And that kind of made me think about it, think about, you know, my prejudices going into reading his report.' "[63]

In the pro-war media and the right-wing blogosphere, the *Lancet* study was treated with vitriol that matched or exceeded the contempt heaped upon Iraq Body Count and Marla Ruzicka. Ironically, some conservatives began treating Iraq Body Count with newfound respect as a source of lower numbers that they could quote against the *Lancet*. Marc Gerlasco's dismissive comment in the *Washington Post* was frequently quoted, even though Gerlasco himself disavowed his comment within days of saying it.[64] "The *Lancet* has become *Al Jazeera* on the Thames,"[65] declared Michael Fumento on the Tech Central Station website. Others called the study "shoddy research," "worthless," "rotten to the core," "obviously bogus on its face . . . a piece of polemical garbage."[66]

The *Lancet* study did not deserve these epithets, but as its authors themselves have stated, its precision was limited. The proper scientific answer to those limitations would be to duplicate the *Lancet* study independently on a larger scale. Not one of the pro-war commentators whose views we have examined (and we have examined many) has ever called for such research. We have not seen a single comment from a supporter of the war suggesting that a better study should be done. For all their fiery attacks on the supposed flaws of the people who are counting the dead, supporters of the war are unable to offer rebuttals in the form of contrary research findings because they haven't attempted to study the question at all. In effect, they have rejected the very idea that the dead in Iraq should be counted.

On December 13, 2005, President Bush for the first time mentioned an estimate of the number of Iraqi deaths. Perhaps it is worth noting that it was the first time the question had ever been posed to him publicly—two and a half years after the war began—and that the person who asked it was not a reporter but a member of an audience to which he had just given a speech. "Since the inception of the Iraqi war, I'd like to know the approximate total of Iraqis who have been killed," the woman asked. "And by Iraqis I include civilians, military, police, insurgents, translators."

Bush responded: "I would say thirty thousand, more or less, have died as a result of the initial incursion and the ongoing violence against Iraqis." White House spokesman Scott McClellan later said that Bush's figure was based on media reports, "not an official government estimate."[67] It was a number that corresponded closely to the figures then current on the Iraq Body Count website. It is remarkably ironic that the president's best sense of the number of dead in his war would come from an antiwar website. And it is not just ironic, but tragic, that even this estimate was probably only a fraction of the real total.

CHAPTER SEVEN

The Mirage of Victory

THE U.S. INVASION OF IRAQ ACCOMPLISHED ONE thing that was indisputably positive: It ended the brutal tyranny of Saddam Hussein. With him fell Iraq's state-controlled media and systems of censorship and repression that had oppressed the nation for decades. "Under Saddam, Iraqi media was like a big advertising company marketing one product called Saddam," said Ahmad Al-Rikaby, a respected Iraqi journalist who had to go into exile during Hussein's rule.[1] The U.S. occupation that replaced Saddam promised freedom, and the people of Iraq began expressing themselves in ways that would have been impossible previously, forming their own newspapers, radio, and other communications media. By November 2003, at least 106 new newspapers had been launched in Baghdad alone. Before the invasion, Iraq was the last country in the Middle East to gain Internet access, and what access people did have was subject to monitoring and censorship. Afterward, Internet cafés began to proliferate, as did weblogs, which—just as they have done in the United States and elsewhere—allowed a cacophony of new voices from Iraq to emerge and express themselves publicly.[2]

One of the first bloggers, who began posting anonymously even before Saddam fell, called himself Salam Pax. Fluent in English, he wrote about his friends, disappearances of people under Saddam Hussein, and conditions in Baghdad as the city braced for war.[3] After the war, his identity was revealed as Salam al-Janabi, a twenty-nine-year-old architect who sometimes worked as a translator for U.S. journalist Peter Maass. His attitude toward the invasion can best be described as complex. His blog displayed a quote from Samuel P. Huntington as its epigram: "The West won the world not by the superiority of its ideas or values or religion but rather by its superiority in applying organized violence. Westerners often forget this fact, non-Westerners never do." During the invasion of Iraq, his blog fell silent for a while, but returned after the fall of Saddam. "War sucks big time," he wrote in his first comments upon his return. "Don't let yourself ever be talked into having one waged in the name of your freedom. Somehow when the bombs start dropping or you hear the sound of machine guns at the end of your street you don't think about your 'imminent liberation' anymore."[4]

Al-Janabi was ecstatic, however, when the dictatorship fell. "The truth is, if it weren't for intervention this would never have happened," he wrote. "When we were watching the Saddam statue being pulled down, one of my aunts was saying that she never thought she would see this day during her lifetime."[5] In response to a query from a U.S. soldier, he wrote, "Saddam is gone, thanks to you. Was it worth it? Be assured it was. We all know that it got to a point where we would have never been rid of Saddam without foreign intervention; I just wish it would have been a bit better planned."[6]

Under U.S. occupation, a range of Iraqi weblogs sprang up, some in English, that offered a range of opinions about the country's politics and the U.S. occupation. Raed Jarrar, a friend of Salam Pax and a critic of the occupation, started a blog called Raed in the Middle. His mother started one called A Family in Baghdad. One of the earliest antioccupation weblogs, written by a Sunni woman in her twenties, was titled Baghdad Burning. (She also created a separate blog about Iraqi cooking, titled Is Something Burning?) From a pro-occupation perspective, there were Healing Iraq, Iraq at a Glance, the Messopotamian [*sic*], Hammorabi, and the optimistically named Iraq the Model, written by three brothers named Ali, Mohammed, and Omar Fadhil. Others bloggers were nonpolitical, such as Baghdad Girl, a fourteen-year-old whose postings consisted mostly of photographs of cute kittens.[7] By April 2006, the Iraq Blog Count website listed 198 weblogs.[8]

Several of the pro-occupation bloggers were hopeful that the fall of Saddam would usher in a period of democratic renewal and progress. By 2006, however, a mood of concern if not despair had begun to set in. The December 2005 elections, hailed by the Bush administration as proof that democracy was taking hold in Iraq, brought to power a government dominated by Shi-ite fundamentalists. "I think this is the darkest image we have conveyed from Iraq in more than two years but it is a fact that it hasn't been this bad in Iraq ever since the 9th of April 2003 [the date Saddam Hussein's government fell]," commented Omar Fadhil on Iraq the Model. "The general sense of the public opinion in Iraq is that our politicians who we trusted proved to be unqualified for the responsibility. Everyone I meet says he feels betrayed by the politicians who keep frustrating us with their incompetence and internal fighting over power."[9] His brother Ali agreed: "I can't see any real light from the various possibilities ahead of us. I think there were huge violations and a fraud especially in the south and the north. This election will cost Iraq and whoever decides to stand by her side at least 10 more years of suffering."[10]

The mood at other pro-occupation blogs was similarly glum. Alarmed by the increasing pace of terrorist activity, the Mes-sopotamian warned, "The people are boiling and a general con-flagration is just around the corner. A situation might develop which will completely wreck all the gains that have been achieved, and render the situation quite untenable."[11] Another previously pro-occupation blogger wrote: "I completely lost the ambition and hope about a secular Iraq where you can express your feelings and thoughts freely especially the religion, but it seems for the coming three centuries the Islamic acts of behead-ing in the name of God for fundamentalists in Sunnis, and the sadist whipping as a punishment (till death) for Shia will im-prove and continue enthusiastically. And might go further to cutting hands and keeping women inside the houses, who knows what is inside the dirty sick minds of the Islamic politicians. God damn them all. . . . We got out of Saddam's prison and got in a new one with a 'democratic' door."[12]

Alien Nation

Of all the arguments for war with Iraq, the only one not subsequently proven to be based on disinformation was the observation that the people of Iraq deserved something better than the oppression they endured under Saddam Hussein. This, however, was at best a minor element in the case for war. White House planners knew from the outset that the American people would never accept it as sufficient cause to sacrifice American lives. As Paul Wolfowitz said shortly after the fall of Saddam's regime, "The criminal treatment of the Iraqi people . . . is a reason to help the Iraqis but it's not a reason to put American kids' lives at risk, certainly not on the scale we did it."[13] As occupiers, moreover, Americans proved ambivalent about the people they were sent to liberate. When there was a conflict between Iraqi rights and American interests, the rights of Iraqis seemed easy to sacrifice.

The gap between Americans and the people they thought they were liberating was vividly demonstrated in the spring of 2004. On March 31, four American private military contractors were ambushed and killed by guerrillas as they drove through Fallujah. Their bodies were dragged from their vehicle by an angry mob, which mutilated and burned the bodies before stringing two of them up on a bridge. The insurgents made their own video of the attack, and the images were broadcast around the world. The following month, *60 Minutes II* broadcast photographs of prisoner abuse by U.S. soldiers at Abu Ghraib prison—formerly the site of torture and murder under Saddam Hussein. Hundreds of photos documenting the abuse had been provided in January to the U.S. Army Criminal Investigation Command by Sergeant Joseph Darby, who had agonized for a month about the abuse before deciding to blow the whistle on his colleagues. "It violated everything I personally believed in and all I'd been taught about the rules of war," Darby said.[14]

The photos showed naked Iraqi prisoners being forced to engage in simulated oral sex and other sex acts, images of a female soldier grinning and pointing at the genitals of a hooded male prisoner, a man being raped with a light stick, and other prisoners being attacked with dogs, beaten, smeared in feces, and threatened with electrocution. Several detainees had died in captivity.[15] By many accounts, the horrible treatment of Iraqi prisoners by U.S. soldiers had been going on since the occupation began. The Red Cross had investigated prisoner conditions in Iraq and warned U.S. officials a year before the photos from Abu Ghraib became known, but it took Darby's leak to make the story public.[16]

In addition to bringing home the horrors of war, the photos exposed the moral ambivalence of American attitudes toward the Iraqi people. On the one hand, the fact that a lone whistle-blower like Joseph Darby could bring the abuse to public light said something inspiring about the power of American ideals. On the other hand, the photos showed that soldiers such as Lynndie England had not only abused but *enjoyed* abusing prisoners.

And even after the photos were released, many of England's neighbors in her hometown of Fort Ashby, West Virginia, seemed to think she had done nothing wrong. "We just had an eighteen-year-old from round here killed by the Iraqis," a friend of England's father told an Australian newspaper. "We went there to help the jackasses and they started blowing us up. Lynndie didn't kill them, she didn't cut them up. She should have shot some of the suckers." According to Colleen Kesner, another resident of Fort Ashby, "A lot of people here think they ought to just blow up the whole of Iraq. To the country boys here, if you're a different nationality, a different race, you're subhuman. That's the way that girls like Lynndie are raised. . . . Tormenting Iraqis, in her mind, would be no different from shooting a turkey. Every season here you're hunting something. Over there, they're hunting Iraqis."[17]

The photos that Joseph Darby turned over to investigators had been taken by Charles Graner, Lynndie England's lover and the ringleader of the abuse. Apparently Graner was so happy with what he was doing that he wanted mementos. And although there were people who praised Darby's courage for coming forward—including Defense Secretary Donald Rumsfeld, who called him "honorable and responsible"—there were others who called him a traitor. Even in his hometown in Maryland, the *Washington Post* reported that resentment of his action was "so deeply felt that even those who praise him do so only anonymously, or with many reservations."[18] According to his wife, Bernadette Darby, "We did not receive the response I thought we would. People were, they were mean, saying he was a walking dead man. He was walking around with a bull's-eye on his head.

It was, it, it was scary." For their own safety, the Darbys went into protective military custody at an undisclosed location.[19]

Just as Iraq weblogs proliferated following Saddam Hussein's downfall, the war produced a similar trend among American soldiers—"milblogs" through which they wrote about their experiences in Iraq. We visited a number of milblogs in the course of researching this book. Many were eloquent and full of interesting details about the experiences that soldiers faced. We were struck, however, by the general rarity of significant conversations or other personal interactions between soldiers and the Iraqi people. The most common friendly interaction that soldiers described in their journals consisted of passing out candy to children. Interactions with adults were rare and often full of tension.[20]

Although the army officially tried to discourage the practice, soldiers in Iraq began referring to the locals as "hajis"—a term based on the Arabic word for "someone who has made the pilgrimage to Mecca." The term did not convey respect. It was the modern-day equivalent of what "gook" or "Charlie" used to mean in Korea and Vietnam. Iraqi shops and flea markets were called "haji marts"; U.S.-trained Iraqi soldiers were "haji patrols."[21] The use of this term reflects the soldiers' perception that they were surrounded by people whose culture they did not understand, let alone appreciate.

The War at Home

By the fall of 2005, some of the war's supporters in the United States were beginning to waver or abandon their positions. In

November of that year, Donald Rumsfeld made a point of telling a reporter for the *Washington Post* about a prewar memo he had written to the president, outlining twenty-nine different ways the war could go badly. His eagerness to talk about the memo was interpreted as Rumsfeld's way of "putting a little distance" between himself and the war that he oversaw. Other former supporters of the war have also backed off, in less subtle ways:

➤ Colonel Lawrence Wilkerson, who was chief of staff to Secretary of State Colin Powell from 2002 to 2005, came to regret his role in helping Powell prepare his prewar speech to the United Nations. "I wish I had not been involved in it," he said. "I look back on it, and I still say it was the lowest point in my life."[22] In October 2005, Wilkerson participated in a panel discussion hosted by the New America Foundation. "I can go through all the things we listed, from WMD to human rights to—I can go through it—terrorism, but I really can't sit here and tell you . . . why we went to war in Iraq," he said, adding that he had witnessed "four-plus years" of "aberrations, bastardizations, perturbations, changes to the national security decision-making process. What I saw was a cabal between the vice president of the United States, Richard Cheney, and the secretary of defense, Donald Rumsfeld, on critical issues that made decisions that the bureaucracy didn't know were being made. And then when the bureaucracy was presented with the decision to carry them out, it was presented in such a disjointed, incredible way that the bureaucracy often didn't know what it was doing as it moved to carry them out." Of Bush himself, Wilkerson said he is "not versed in international relations and not too interested in them either."[23]

➤ Italian premier Silvio Berlusconi was one of Bush's strongest supporters during the run-up to war. On the eve of the conflict in March 2003, he told Italian lawmakers that using force against Iraq was legitimate and that Italy couldn't abandon the Americans "in their fight against terrorism." In October 2005, however, he declared that he had been against the war all along. "I was never convinced that war was the best system to bring democracy to the country and to get rid of a bloody dictatorship," he said. "I tried several times to convince the American president to not go to war. . . . I believed that military action should have been avoided."[24]

➤ "One can't doubt that the American objective in Iraq has failed," wrote conservative icon William F. Buckley, Jr., in February 2006. President Bush, he said, must "submit to a historical reality" and make "the acknowledgment of defeat."[25]

➤ During the run-up to war in 2002, Democratic Party politicians were divided over Iraq. In October of that year, 126 Democrats in the U.S. House of Representatives voted for a resolution authorizing Bush to go to war, while 133 voted against it. In the Senate, 29 voted for the measure and 21 against. Some of these pro-war votes were simple political opportunism. Democrats feared being seen as opposing a popular president on a national security issue. By the end of

2005, however, the national mood had changed and Democrats who had supported the war began to openly oppose it. Congressman John Murtha, a Vietnam veteran and strong backer of Operation Desert Storm in 1991, had also supported the war in Iraq in 2002 and 2003, and as the country spiraled into chaos, his first impulse was to call for increasing troop levels. By November 2005, however, he had had enough. "The war in Iraq is not going as advertised," he said. "It is a flawed policy wrapped in illusion. The American public is way ahead of us. . . . Our military has done everything that has been asked of them, the U.S. can not accomplish anything further in Iraq militarily. It is time to bring them home."[26]

White House insiders reported that Bush himself was frustrated, angry, and bitter. "He's like the lion in winter," a political friend of Bush told New York *Daily News* reporter Thomas M. DeFrank. "He's frustrated. He remains quite confident in the decisions he has made. But this is a guy who wanted to do big things in a second term. Given his nature, there's no way he'd be happy about the way things have gone." Another source with close ties to the White House said he was losing his temper with aides. "The president is just unhappy in general and casting blame all about," said one Bush insider. "Andy [Card, the chief of staff] gets his share. Karl [Rove] gets his share. Even Cheney gets his share. And the press gets a big share." Bush is so dismayed that "the only person escaping blame is the president himself," said a sympathetic official, who politely termed such self-exoneration "illogical."[27]

Exit Strategy

The three most significant U.S. wars since 1945—Korea, Vietnam, and now Iraq—share an important trait: as casualties mounted, American public support declined. This has happened even more rapidly in Iraq than in past wars. In the past, these falloffs in public support have proved irreversible, and there is little reason to imagine that Iraq will be different. By March 2006, a Gallup survey found that three out of four Americans thought a civil war was either likely to occur in Iraq or was already occurring. Only 44 percent of Americans believed the U.S. would win the war, and 55 percent said the decision to go to war had been a mistake. Two-thirds of Americans favored withdrawing some or all U.S. troops.[28] With the exception of minor and temporary fluctuations, these numbers were essentially unchanged from those of six months previously, when pollster Daniel Yankelovich reported that the public was approaching a "tipping point": the moment when "large swaths of the public begin to demand that the government address their concerns." Barring unforeseen circumstances, Yankelovich estimated that "the Bush administration has about a year before the public's impatience will force it to change course."[29] Yet by the most optimistic estimates of administration officials, the U.S. will need five to ten years to achieve its objectives in Iraq.

It is no longer a question, in our opinion, of *whether* the U.S. will be forced to pull out of Iraq. The question is *when* it will happen, and it's hard to imagine that we will leave Iraq in better shape than when we went in. We need to face these facts and figure out

how to deal with them, because we will be dealing with the consequences of the mess in Iraq for a long time into the future.

One way of dealing with the mess would be for the United
States to withdraw into isolationism—an approach that has
some precedent in American history. Declining support for the
war in Iraq has indeed produced a revival of isolationist thinking. In fall 2005, a survey by the Pew Research Center and the
Council on Foreign Relations found that 42 percent of Americans say the United States should "mind its own business inter-
nationally and let other countries get along the best they can on
their own"—up from 30 percent in 2002, and marking a return
"to levels not seen since post–Cold War 1990s and the post–
Vietnam 1970s." In fact, reported Pew analyst Andrew Kohut,
"In more than 40 years of polling only in 1976 and 1995 did
public opinion tilt this far toward isolationism."[30]

Isolationism, however, is not an option in today's world, with
its dense network of economic, cultural, and even electronic in-
terconnections. It is particularly unlikely to be an option for the
United States as long as America aspires to remain a world superpower. The mistakes made in Iraq—the faulty intelligence,
indifference to the war's impact on the Iraqi people—are partly
a consequence of the propaganda used to sell the war, but that
propaganda and Americans' willingness to believe it are largely a
reflection of the contradictory impulses—isolationism and
interventionism—that define our relationship with the rest of
the world. Americans cannot continue to have it both ways.

Critics of the U.S. war in Iraq have often pointed to the con-
tradiction between the idealism of America's stated objectives—
democracy, peace, freedom—and the sordid realities of war,

human rights abuses, and corruption. Less frequently noted is the fundamental *incoherence* of U.S. policy, not just in Iraq under the Bush administration, but throughout the Middle East and for decades. To illustrate this point, here is a short list of some major episodes in American involvement:

➤ In the 1950s, the United States followed the lead of the British in supporting the overthrow of the Mossadegh government in Iran. The British motive in this incident was clear: a desire to retain control of Iranian oil. The United States, however, got snookered. Americans accepted British claims that Mossadegh (a democrat and civil libertarian) was a closet socialist and treated Iran as a turf battle in the Cold War.

➤ The 1979 Islamic revolution in Iran prompted alarm in Washington, which reacted throughout the 1980s by supporting the government of Saddam Hussein during the Iran/Iraq war. For policymakers during this period, Hussein's Baathist regime (even though it professed socialist leanings and had a history of ties to the Soviet Union) was seen as a bulwark against the spread of Iran's Shiite fundamentalism.

➤ Iraq's 1990 invasion of Kuwait sparked a reversal in U.S. policy. Almost overnight, Hussein went from being an ally to "worse than Hitler," and the United States led Operation Desert Storm to drive him out of Kuwait, followed by a decade of sanctions as well as military and political efforts to overthrow his regime.

➤ Notwithstanding the tilt against Iraq, after Operation Desert Storm, U.S. troops allowed Saddam Hussein to quell an uprising by Iraq's Shiite majority population. The U.S. thus enabled Saddam to remain in power, largely out of fear of becoming embroiled in a quagmire, combined with fear of Shiite advances that would benefit Iran.

➤ In 2003, the United States invaded Iraq, overthrew Saddam Hussein's regime, and paved the way for elections that brought a Shiite fundamentalist government to power in Iraq, which is expected to form friendly ties with Iran.

Each of these twists and turns in policy has been accompanied by a combination of triumphal rhetoric about America's lofty aims and dire warnings about the consequences that will follow if America fails to act. Each time, the proponents of these policies have argued that the United States must intervene and win, and that victory will transform the Middle East into an oasis of democracy and peace. Yet each step toward that victory has ended in disappointment, followed by new plans for new interventions, accompanied by new promises that the oasis of victory is directly ahead. After several decades of wandering in this desert, perhaps the time has come to recognize that America has been chasing a mirage—an image that is based more on its own wishful thinking than on any realistic understanding of the region it seeks to lead.

As this book neared completion, American politicians and pundits had begun to talk about attacking *Iran*, using rhetoric very similar to the arguments that led to the current quagmire in

Iraq. We can only hope that the American people remember how badly they were misled the last time they were told that pre-emptive aggression was necessary to neutralize an "imminent threat" in the Middle East. Expanding the war from Iraq into Iran would be madness.

Rather than an expansion of the war, we believe that public disillusionment and the growing civil war in Iraq will eventually force U.S. policymakers to withdraw American troops. When this happens, we can expect to hear a new round of rationalizations about the reasons for the latest failure to bring stability and democracy to the region. Some of those arguments are already beginning to be aired:

➤ *"If only the occupation had been planned better, it might have succeeded."* The absence of planning, however, is itself a consequence of the propaganda that was used to sell the war. Repeatedly, when faced with predictions of problems, White House officials dismissed the warnings of Iraq experts and adopted plans that were unrealistic because of their optimism—too few troops on the ground to maintain security; failure to anticipate the insurgency; oblivious disregard, even disdain, for those who attempted to assess the human and economic costs of war. These warnings went unheeded because giving them credence would have undermined the public relations effort to sell the war to the American people.

➤ *"We didn't really fight to win."* This argument was aired in February 2006 by *Weekly Standard* editor William Kristol.

"We have not had a serious three-year effort to fight a war in Iraq," Kristol said on Fox News.[31] Kristol had been one of its most ardent proponents of war with Iraq, and during earlier stages of the occupation, he had said that "it's going pretty well. . . . I'm actually somewhat heartened. I was a little worried that the administration was a little slow in the sort of reconstruction of Iraq, but I think they're getting it together pretty well."[32]

➤ *"The liberals betrayed us."* This argument is also beginning to circulate among conservative pundits. It is true, of course, that many liberals in the United States opposed the war with Iraq, and even more have come to believe that it is unwinnable. However, it is especially ridiculous to blame liberals for the outcome of the Iraq war when they had no hand in planning it. The war with Iraq was conceived, planned, and executed by an unabashedly conservative president with almost unprecedented ability to act unencumbered by concern for the wishes of his political opponents. Throughout the course of the war, the Republican Party has controlled every branch of the United States government—the White House, both houses of Congress, and the judiciary. They surely are the ones who must be considered responsible for the consequences of their actions.

In seeking alternatives to the disastrous course of recent history, we must begin by holding accountable the public officials who actually sold these policies to the American people. It may not always be clear which officials intentionally deceived the public, and which ones merely repeated falsehoods that were told to them by others. The question of whether they were liars or fools, however, is less important than the question of whether they have shown themselves qualified to lead. Clearly, they have not. The evidence shows irrefutably that lies were told by *someone*. The public has an absolute right to expect that government officials will find their way to the truth and lead accordingly, and America's current leadership has demonstrated repeatedly that it either cannot or will not do so. If it remains in power, we cannot expect better in the future.

Notes

Although most of the sources cited for this book are traditional books, newspapers and similar print documents, we have tried whenever possible to supply an internet URL so that interested readers can find the full text of the document cited. In some cases we have provided URLs to websites that have republished articles which are not available (or are available only for a fee) on the original publisher's website. Unless otherwise indicated, all URLs listed below were visited between the dates of December 1, 2005, and April 15, 2006. Some URLs are bound to become obsolete over time, but many deleted web pages can still be found on the Internet Archive, http://www.archive.org.

Introduction: **The Innocents Abroad**

1. Evan Thomas, John Barry, and Christian Caryl, "A War in the Dark," *Newsweek*, November 10, 2003, p. 24, http://www.msnbc.msn.com/id/3339591/site/newsweek/.
2. Greg Jaffe, "In Iraq, One Officer Uses Cultural Skills to Fight Insurgents," *Wall Street Journal*, November 15, 2005, p. A1, http://aimpoints.hq.af.mil/display.cfm?id=7816.

3. Tom DeLay, interview by John Gibson, *The Big Story with John Gibson* (transcript), August 21, 2002.

4. Sheldon Rampton and John Stauber, *Weapons of Mass Deception: The Uses of Propaganda in Bush's War on Iraq* (New York: Tarcher/Penguin, 2003), p. 7.

5. Gregory Fontenot, L. J. Degen, and David Tohn, "Regime Collapse," in *On Point: The United States Army in Operation Iraqi Freedom* (Fort Leavenworth, KS: Center for Army Lessons Learned, U.S. Army Combined Arms Center, 2004), http://call.army.mil/products/on-point/toc.asp.

6. Aparisim Ghosh, "The Last Days of Bush's Viceroy," *Time*, June 25, 2004.

7. *Dateline NBC*, "Bremer's War" (transcript), January 8, 2006.

Chapter One: **The Victory of Spin**

1. National Security Council, *National Strategy for Victory in Iraq*, November 2005, http://www.whitehouse.gov/infocus/iraq/iraq_national_strategy_20051130.pdf.

2. Peter Baker, "Bush Brings More Realistic View of War to Forefront," *Washington Post*, December 19, 2005, p. A1, http://www.washingtonpost.com/wp-dyn/content/article/2005/12/18/AR2005121801308.html.

3. George W. Bush, "President's Address to the Nation" (televised address), December 18, 2005, http://www.whitehouse.gov/news/releases/2005/12/20051218-2.html.

4. George W. Bush, "President Bush Announces Combat Operations in Iraq Have Ended" (transcript of speech given aboard the USS *Abraham Lincoln*), May 1, 2003, http://www.state.gov/p/nea/rls/rm/20203.htm.

5. Scott Shane, "Bush's Speech on Iraq Echoes Analyst's Voice," *New York Times*, December 4, 2005, p. 1.

6. National Security Council, *National Strategy for Victory in Iraq*.

7. David W. Moore, "Americans Skeptical Bush Has 'Victory' Plan," Gallup News Service, December 1, 2005, http://poll.gallup.com/content/default.aspx?ci=20224.

8. David W. Moore, "Most Americans Say Bush Has No Clear Plan for

Iraq," Gallup News Service, March 14, 2006, http://poll.gallup.com/content/default.aspx?ci=21907.

9. George Packer, "War After the War," *New Yorker*, November 24, 2003, http://www.newyorker.com/fact/content/?031124fa_fact1.

10. David L. Phillips, "Losing Iraq: Inside the Postwar Reconstruction Fiasco" (speech transcript), Carnegie Council on Ethics and International Affairs, April 27, 2005, http://www.carnegiecouncil.org/viewMedia.php/prmTemplateID/8/prmID/5161.

11. Sheldon Rampton and John Stauber, "Weapons of Mass Deception," March 9, 2003, http://www.sourcewatch.org/index.php?title=Weapons_of_mass_deception&oldid=8. (This essay, posted on our website, became the seed of our later book of the same title.)

12. *Guardian* (UK), "Survey: What the World Thinks of America," October 15, 2004, http://www.guardian.co.uk/uselections2004/viewsofamerica. Leticia Juárez G., "Mexico, the United States and the War in Iraq," *International Journal of Public Opinion Research*, 16, no. 3 (2004): 331–343, http://ijpor.oxfordjournals.org/cgi/content/abstract/16/3/331.

13. Pew Research Center for the People and the Press, "America's Image Further Erodes, Europeans Want Weaker Ties," March 18, 2003, http://people-press.org/reports/display.php3?ReportID=175.

14. Pew Research Center for the People and the Press, "A Year After Iraq War," March 16, 2004, http://people-press.org/reports/display.php3?ReportID=206.

15. James Zogby, "Attitudes of Arabs 2005," Arab American Institute, December 2005, http://www.aaiusa.org/PDF/2005%20Arab%20Poll.pdf.

16. Frank Luntz, "Communicating the Principles of Prevention and Protection in the War on Terror" (memo), June 2004, http://www.sourcewatch.org/images/2/2f/Luntz.pdf.

17. Jay Price, "Soldiers Get Tips on Dealing with Media," *News & Observer* (Raleigh, NC), January 10, 2005, p. A1.

18. Michael Keane, "Our Tortured Language of War," *Los Angeles Times*, January 18, 2005, p. B13.

19. Hearing of the Defense Subcommittee of the House Appropriations Committee, Chaired by Rep. Jerry Lewis, U.S. Congress, Federal News Service, March 27, 2003.

20. Robert Collier, "Oil Firms Wait as Iraq Crisis Unfolds," *San Francisco Chronicle*, September 29, 2002, http://www.sfgate.com/cgi-bin/article.cgi?file=/chronicle/archive/2002/09/29/MN116803.DTL.

21. Associated Press, "Iraq's Oil Exports Hit Lowest Level Since War; Oil Minister Resigns," January 3, 2006, http://www.usatoday.com/news/world/iraq/2006-01-03-fuel-crisis_x.htm.

22. "Occupying Iraq: Is the Cost, in Blood and Money, Too High?" *Economist*, August 7, 2003, http://www.economist.com/world/africa/displayStory.cfm?story_id=1974616&no_na_tran=1.

23. Amy Belasco, *The Cost of Iraq, Afghanistan and Enhanced Base Security Since 9/11*, Congressional Research Service report, October 7, 2005, p. 7, http://www.opencrs.com/rpts/RL33110_20051007.pdf.

24. Jamie Wilson, "Iraq War Could Cost U.S. Over $2 Trillion, Says Nobel Prize–Winning Economist," *Guardian* (UK), January 7, 2006. Linda Bilmes and Joseph Stiglitz, "The Economic Costs of the Iraq War: An Appraisal Three Years After the Beginning of the Conflict" (paper prepared for presentation at the annual meeting of the Allied Social Science Associations, Boston), January 8, 2006, http://www2.gsb.columbia.edu/faculty/jstiglitz/Cost_of_War_in_Iraq.pdf.

25. Eric Schmitt, "Army Chief Raises Estimate of G.I.'s Needed in Postwar Iraq," *New York Times*, February 25, 2003, http://www.nytimes.com/2003/02/25/international/middleeast/25CND-MILI.html?ex=1136696400&en=cc74abe68aaed29c&ei=5070.

26. *Department of Defense Budget Priorities for Fiscal Year 2004*, Hearing before the Committee on the Budget, House of Representatives, 108th Congress, Washington, D.C., February 27, 2003, U.S. Government Printing Office, Serial No. 108–6, http://frwebgate.access.gpo.gov/cgi-bin/getdoc.cgi?dbname=108_house_hearings&docid=f:85421.pdf.

27. *Results in Iraq: 100 Days Toward Security and Freedom*, White House report, August 8, 2003, p. 5, http://www.whitehouse.gov/infocus/iraq/100days/100days.pdf.

28. Reuters, "CIA Report Finds No Zarqawi-Saddam Link," October 6, 2004, http://www.msnbc.msn.com/id/6189795.

29. Richard Burkholder, "Ousting Saddam Hussein 'Was Worth Hardships Endured Since Invasion,' Say Citizens of Baghdad," Gallup survey

report, September 23, 2003, http://brain.gallup.com/content/default.aspx
?ci=9334.

30. Dana Milbank and Mike Allen, "U.S. Effort Aims to Improve Opinions About Iraq Conflict," *Washington Post*, September 30, 2004, p. A20, http://www.washingtonpost.com/wp-dyn/articles/A60725-2004Sep29
.html.

31. Sean Aday, Steven Livingston, and Maeve Hebert, "Embedding the Truth: A Cross-Cultural Analysis of Objectivity and Television Coverage of the Iraq War," *Harvard International Journal of Press/Politics* 10, no. 1 (2005): 11–12, 18, http://www.gwu.edu/~smpa/faculty/documents/
EmbeddingTheTruth.pdf.

32. James Rainey, "Portraits of War," *Los Angeles Times*, May 21, 2005, p. A1, http://www.latimes.com/news/nationworld/iraq/la-na-iraq photo21
may21,1,107258.story?page=1&coll=la-util-nationworld-world.

33. Farnaz Fassihi, e-mail to friends, September 24, 2004, http://www
.commondreams.org/views04/0930-15.htm. Also see Farnaz Fassihi, "Baghdad Diary," *Columbia Journalism Review*, November/December 2004, http://www.cjr.org/issues/2004/6/fassihi-baghdad.asp.

34. Greg Mitchell, "Will 'WSJ' Reporter Who Wrote Famous E-mail on Horrid Conditions in Iraq Lose Her Beat?" *Editor and Publisher*, October 4, 2004, http://www.editorandpublisher.com/eandp/article_brief/eandp/
1/1000653017.

35. George W. Bush, "President Discusses War on Terror and Operation Iraqi Freedom" (transcript of speech given at the Renaissance Cleveland Hotel), March 20, 2006, http://www.whitehouse.gov/news/releases/2006/
03/20060320-7.html.

36. U.S. Department of Defense, *Information Operations Roadmap*, October 30, 2003, p. 26, http://www.gwu.edu/~nsarchiv/NSAEBB/NSAEBB
177/info_ops_roadmap.pdf.

37. "Air Force Intelligence and Security Doctrine: Psychological Operations (PSYOP)," Air Force Instruction 10-702, Secretary of the Air Force, July 19, 1994, http://www.fas.org/irp/doddir/usaf/10-702.htm.

38. Mark Mazzetti, "PR Meets Psy-Ops in War on Terror," *Los Angeles Times*, December 1, 2004, p. A1.

39. Tony Sanders, "Talkers Take Their Trade to Iraq," *Billboard Radio*

Monitor, April 22, 2005, http://www.billboardradiomonitor.com/radio monitor/search/article_display.jsp?vnu_content_id=1000893455.

40. Move America Forward, "Move America Forward and Talk Radio Are Moving to Baghdad!" July 2005, http://www.moveamericaforward.org/index.php/MAF/CurrentProject/the_truth_tour_live_from_baghdad/.

41. Kelley Beaucar Vlahos, "Critics Call Radio Hosts' Trip Propaganda Mission," *Fox News*, July 6, 2005, http://www.foxnews.com/story/0,2933, 161463,00.html.

42. *O'Dwyer's Public Relations News*, "U.S. Plans Iraq PR Push," September 16, 2004, http://www.odwyerpr.com/members/archived_stories _2004/september/0916iraqpr.htm.

43. *O'Dwyer's Public Relations News*, "U.S. Force Taps PR Help for Iraq," September 30, 2004, http://www.odwyerpr.com/members/archived _stories_2004/september/0930iraq.htm.

44. Jeff Gerth, "Military's Information War Is Vast and Often Secretive," *New York Times*, December 11, 2005, p. 1.

45. David S. Cloud, "Quick Rise for Purveyors of Propaganda in Iraq," *New York Times*, February 15, 2006, http://www.nytimes.com/2006/02/ 15/politics/15lincoln.html.

46. Renae Merle, "Pentagon Funds Diplomacy Effort," *Washington Post*, June 11, 2005, p. D1, http://www.washingtonpost.com/wp-dyn/ content/article/2005/06/10/AR2005061001910.html.

47. Mark Mazzetti and Borzou Daragahi, "U.S. Military Covertly Pays to Run Stories in Iraqi Press," *Los Angeles Times*, November 30, 2005, http://www.latimes.com/news/nationworld/world/la-fg-infowar30nov30, 0,5638790.story.

48. Ibid.

49. Gerth, "Military's Information War."

50. "Military Journalist Helps Iraqi Reporters Improve Skills," *Soldier Stories*, March 17, 2004, http://www4.army.mil/ocpa/soldierstories/story .php?story_id_key=5753.

51. Rick Jervis and Zaid Sabah, "Probe into Iraq Coverage Widens," *USA Today*, December 9, 2005, http://www.usatoday.com/news/world/ iraq/2005-12-08-media-probe_x.htm.

52. U.S.Government Accountability Office, *Opinion B-229257*, June 10, 1988, http://redbook.gao.gov/13/fl0060205.php.

53. Josh White, "Military Planting Articles in Iraq Papers," *Washington Post*, December 1, 2005, p.A18, http://www.washingtonpost.com/wp-dyn/content/article/2005/11/30/AR2005113001876.html.

54. Associated Press, "Congress, Rumsfeld Want Answers on Press Propaganda in Iraq," November 30, 2005, http://www.editorandpublisher.com/eandp/news/article_display.jsp?vnu_content_id=1001612485.

55. Donald Rumsfeld, interview by Charlie Rose, *The Charlie Rose Show* (transcript released by the U.S. Defense Department), February 17, 2006, http://www.defenselink.mil/transcripts/2006/tr20060217-12553.html.

56. Defense Department operational update briefing with Secretary of Defense Donald Rumsfeld and General Peter Pace (transcript), February 21, 2006, http://www.jcs.mil/chairman/speeches/060221SecDefPressBrief.html.

57. Department of Defense news briefing with General George Casey (transcript), March 3, 2006, http://www.mnf-iraq.com/Transcripts/060303.htm.

58. Gerth, "Military's Information War."

59. Paul McLeary, "Wherein We Learn More of the Propaganda Machine," CJR Daily (weblog), December 12, 2005, http://www.cjrdaily.org/politics/wherein_we_learn_more_of_the_p.php.

60. Mark Mazzetti and Kevin Sack, "Planted PR Stories Not News to Military," *Los Angeles Times*, December 18, 2005, http://www.latimes.com/news/nationworld/nation/la-na-infowar18dec18,0,1826110.story.

Chapter Two: **The Plame Game**

1. "President Bush—Job Ratings," PollingReport.com, http://www.pollingreport.com/BushJob1.htm. See also David W. Moore, "Bush Job Approval Reflects 'Rally Effect,'" Gallup News Service, September 18, 2001, http://poll.gallup.com/content/default.aspx?ci=4912&pg=1.

2. *CBS News*, "Poll: U.S. Losing Control in Iraq," July 10, 2003, http://www.cbsnews.com/stories/2003/07/10/opinion/polls/main562628.shtml.

3. Jeffrey M. Jones, "Bush Finishes 19th Quarter in Office on Low

Note," Gallup News Service, October 21, 2005, http://poll.gallup.com/content/default.aspx?ci=19363&pg=1.

4. George W. Bush, State of the Union address, January 28, 2003, http://www.whitehouse.gov/news/releases/2003/01/20030128-19.html.

5. Seymour M. Hersh, "Who Lied to Whom?" *New Yorker*, March 31, 2003, p. 41, http://www.newyorker.com/archive/content/?030714fr_archive02.

6. Select Committee on Intelligence, United States Senate, *Report on the U.S. Intelligence Community's Prewar Intelligence Assessments on Iraq*, July 18, 2004, pp. 37–38, http://www.factcheck.org/UploadedFiles/US%20Report.pdf.

7. Tom Hamburger, Peter Wallsten, and Bob Drogin, "French Told CIA of Bogus Intelligence," *Los Angeles Times*, December 11, 2005, http://fairuse.1accesshost.com/news2/latimes975.html.

8. Dana Priest and Dana Milbank, "President Defends Allegation on Iraq," *Washington Post*, July 15, 2003, p. A1, http://www.washingtonpost.com/ac2/wp-dyn?pagename=article&contentId=A56336-2003Jul14.

9. Joseph C. Wilson IV, *The Politics of Truth: Inside the Lies that Led to War and Betrayed My Wife's CIA Identity* (New York: Carroll & Graf, 2004), p. 153.

10. Richard Leiby and Walter Pincus, "Ex-Envoy: Nuclear Report Ignored," *Washington Post*, July 6, 2003, http://www.commondreams.org/headlines03/0706-05.htm.

11. Joseph C. Wilson IV, "What I Didn't Find in Africa," *New York Times*, July 6, 2003, http://www.commondreams.org/views03/0706-02.htm.

12. Bureau of Intelligence and Research, U.S. State Department, *Niger-Iraq: Sale of Niger Uranium to Iraq Unlikely*, March 4, 2002, http://www.judicialwatch.org/archive/niger-uranium.pdf.

13. Select Committee on Intelligence, United States Senate, *Prewar Intelligence Assessments on Iraq*, pp. 49–50, 58, 61–62.

14. Condoleezza Rice, "Why We Know Iraq Is Lying," *New York Times*, January 23, 2003, p. A25.

15. Select Committee, *Prewar Intelligence Assessments on Iraq*, pp. 49–50, 58, 61–62.

16. Bush, State of the Union Address, 2003.

17. Mohamed ElBaradei, *Status of the Agency's Verification Activities in Iraq As of 8 January 2003*, International Atomic Energy Agency, January 9, 2003, http://www.iaea.org/NewsCenter/Statements/2003/ebsp2003n 002.shtml.

18. Mohamed ElBaradei, "Q&A with the Top Sleuth" (interview), *Time*, January 20, 2003, p. 44.

19. Mohamed ElBaradei, interview with Gwen Ifill, *NewsHour with Jim Lehrer* (transcript), January 28, 2003, http://www.pbs.org/newshour/bb/international/jan-june03/elbaradei_1-28.html.

20. Hersh, "Who Lied to Whom?"

21. Mohamed ElBaradei, *The Status of Nuclear Inspections in Iraq: An Update*, statement to the United Nations Security Council, March 7, 2003, http://www.iaea.org/NewsCenter/Statements/2003/ebsp2003n006.shtml.

22. *Meet the Press*, "Vice President Dick Cheney Discusses a Possible War with Iraq," March 16, 2003.

23. Romesh Ratnesar, "His Lonely March," *Time*, March 17, 2003, p. 20.

24. Henry Waxman, letter to President George W. Bush, March 17, 2003, http://www.fas.org/irp/news/2003/03/waxman.pdf.

25. Vicky Ward, "Double Exposure," *Vanity Fair*, January 2004, http://www.vanityfair.com/commentary/content/articles/051010roco03d.

26. Joseph Wilson, interview by CNN, March 8, 2003, http://transcripts.cnn.com/TRANSCRIPTS/0303/08/cst.07.html.

27. Nicholas Kristof, "Why Truth Matters," *New York Times*, May 6, 2003, http://www.cnn.com/2003/US/05/06/nyt.kristof/.

28. *Meet the Press*, "Condoleezza Rice Discusses Middle East Peace and Iraq" (transcript), June 8, 2003.

29. Wilson, "What I Didn't Find in Africa."

30. David E. Sanger, "Bush Claim on Iraq Had Flawed Source, White House Says," *New York Times*, August 8, 2003, p. A1.

31. Ari Fleischer, White House daily press briefing (transcript), July 7, 2003.

32. George J. Tenet, *Statement by George J. Tenet, Director of Central Intelligence*, July 11, 2003, http://www.cia.gov/cia/public_affairs/press _release/2003/pr07112003.html.

33. Michael Isikoff and Tamara Lipper, "A Spy Takes the Bullet," *Newsweek*, July 21, 2003, p. 24.

34. James Risen, "Bush Aides Now Say Claim on Uranium Was Accurate," *New York Times*, July 14, 2003, p. A7, http://www.nytimes.com/2003/07/14/international/worldspecial/14INTE.html.

35. Mark Matthews, "Bush Aide Admits Fault on Iraq Try for Uranium," *Baltimore Sun*, July 23, 2003, http://www.baltimoresun.com/news/nationworld/iraq/bal-te.uranium23jul23,0,5767493.story?coll=bal-iraq-headlines.

36. Condoleezza Rice, interview by Gwen Ifill, *Newshour with Jim Lehrer* (transcript), July 30, 2003, http://www.pbs.org/newshour/bb/white_house/july-dec03/rice_7-30.html.

37. George Bush, "President Bush Discusses Top Priorities for the U.S." (press conference transcript), July 30, 2003, http://www.whitehouse.gov/news/releases/2003/07/20030730-1.html.

38. Walter Pincus and Jim VandeHei, "Plame's Identity Marked as Secret," *Washington Post*, July 21, 2005, p. A1, http://www.washingtonpost.com/wp-dyn/content/article/2005/07/20/AR2005072002517.html.

39. U.S. Department of Justice, "White House Official I. Lewis Libby Indicted on Obstruction of Justice, False Statement and Perjury Charges Relating to Leak of Classified Information Revealing CIA Officer's Identity" (news release), October 28, 2005, http://www.usdoj.gov/usao/iln/osc/documents/libby_pr_28102005.pdf.

40. Judith Miller, "My Four Hours Testifying in the Federal Grand Jury Room," *New York Times*, October 16, 2005, p. 31, http://www.commondreams.org/headlines05/1016-01.htm.

41. Ibid.

42. Bob Woodward, "Testifying in the CIA Leak Case," *Washington Post*, November 16, 2005, p. A8, http://www.washingtonpost.com/wp-dyn/content/article/2005/11/15/AR2005111501829_pf.html.

43. CNN, "Cheney's Top Aide Indicted," October 29, 2005, http://www.cnn.com/2005/POLITICS/10/28/leak.probe. See also Pete Yost, "Mysterious 'Official A' Is Karl Rove," Associated Press, October 28, 2005, http://www.truthout.org/docs_2005/103105X.shtml.

44. *United States of America v. I. Lewis Libby*, statement of indictment, October 28, 2005, p. 8, http://www.usdoj.gov/usao/iln/osc/documents/libby_indictment_28102005.pdf.

45. Matt Cooper, "What I Told the Grand Jury," *Time*, July 25, 2005,

p. 38. See also "Matt Cooper: Interview with *Time* Reporter" (transcript), *Good Morning America*, October 31, 2005.

46. *United States of America v. I. Lewis Libby*.

47. Walter Pincus, "Anonymous Sources: Their Use in a Time of Prosecutorial Interest," *Nieman Watchdog*, July 6, 2005, http://www.niemanwatchdog .org/index.cfm?fuseaction=Showcase.view&showcaseid=0019.

48. Robert Novak, "The Mission to Niger," *Chicago Sun-Times*, July 14, 2003, p. 31, http://www.townhall.com/opinion/columns/robertnovak/ 2003/07/14/160881.html.

49. Evan Thomas and Michael Isikoff, "Secrets and Leaks," *Newsweek*, July 12, 2005, http://msnbc.msn.com/id/3129861.

50. "The O'Reilly Factor" Fox News (transcript), July 12, 2005, http:// www.foxnews.com/story/0,2933,162394,00.html.

51. Clifford D. May, "Scandal!" *National Review*, July 11, 2003, http:// www.nationalreview.com/may/may071103.asp.

52. "Did White House Leak Name of Undercover CIA Employee?" *CNN Crossfire* (transcript), September 29, 2003, http://transcripts.cnn .com/TRANSCRIPTS/0309/29/cf.00.html.

53. Letter from Stanley M. Moskowitz, Director of Congressional Affairs, U.S. Central Intelligence Agency, to Congressman John Conyers, Jr., January 30, 2004, http://www.house.gov/judiciary_democrats/ cialeakinforesp13004.pdf.

54. David Corn, "A White House Smear," *Nation*, July 16, 2003, http:// www.thenation.com/blogs/capitalgames?bid=3&pid=823.

55. Shaun Waterman, "Commentary: Message Over Medium?" United Press International, October 5, 2003, http://www.upi.com/inc/view.php ?StoryID=20031005-083619-1370r.

56. Scott McClellan, White House press briefing (transcript), September 16, 2003, http://www.whitehouse.gov/news/releases/2003/09/ 20030916-6.html.

57. Scott McClellan, White House press briefing (transcript), September 29, 2003, http://www.whitehouse.gov/news/releases/2003/09/ 20030929-7.html.

58. George W. Bush, "President Discusses Job Creation with Business Leaders" (transcript), September 30, 2003, http://www.whitehouse.gov/ news/releases/2003/09/20030930-9.html.

59. *United States of America v. I. Lewis Libby.*

60. Select Committee, *Prewar Intelligence Assessments on Iraq,* pp. 44–46.

61. Committee of Privy Counselors, House of Commons, *Review of Intelligence on Weapons of Mass Destruction,* July 14, 2004, p. 123, http://www .archive2.official-documents.co.uk/document/deps/hc/hc898/898.pdf.

62. Charles Duelfer, *Comprehensive Report of the Special Advisor to the DCI on Iraq's WMD,* September 30, 2004, http://www.cia.gov/cia/ reports/iraq_wmd_2004/chap4.html.

63. R. Jeffrey Smith, "Bush Authorized Secrets' Release, Libby Testified," *Washington Post,* April 7, 2006, p. A1, http://www.washingtonpost .com/wp-dyn/content/article/2006/04/06/AR2006040600333.html.

64. Scott McClellan, White House press briefing, April 7, 2006, http:// www.whitehouse.gov/news/releases/2006/04/20060407-3.html.

Chapter Three: **Big Impact**

1. George W. Bush, State of the Union address, January 28, 2003, http://www.whitehouse.gov/news/releases/2003/01/20030128-19.html.

2. Colin Powell, "U.S. Secretary of State Colin Powell Addresses the UN Security Council," February 5, 2003, http://www.whitehouse.gov/ news/releases/2003/02/20030205-1.html.

3. Gilbert Cranberg, "Bring Back the Skeptical Press," *Washington Post,* June 29, 2003, p. B2, http://www.washingtonpost.com/ac2/wp-dyn/ A43586-2003Jun27.

4. *New York Times,* "The Case Against Iraq" (editorial), February 6, 2003, p. A38; and Steven R. Weisman, "Powell, in U.N. Speech, Presents Case to Show Iraq Has Not Disarmed," *New York Times,* February 6, 2003, p. A1.

5. Michael R. Gordon, "Powell's Trademark: Overwhelm Them," *New York Times,* February 6, 2003, p. A1.

6. *Washington Post,* "Irrefutable" (editorial), February 6, 2003, p. A36.

7. *Los Angeles Times,* "U.N. — Time for a Deadline" (editorial), February 6, 2003, part 2, p. 16.

8. *Washington Times*, "Smoking Intercepts" (editorial), February 6, 2003, p. A2.

9. *Dallas Morning News*, "Only the Blind Could Ignore Powell's Evidence" (editorial), February 6, 2003, p. 18A.

10. *San Francisco Chronicle*, "A Strong Case, But for War?" (editorial), February 6, 2003, p. A22.

11. *Denver Post*, "U.N. Should Heed Powell" (editorial), February 6, 2003, p. B6.

12. United Press International, "What U.S. Newspapers Are Saying," February 8, 2003.

13. *Washington Times*, "Smoking Intercepts."

14. Bruce B. Auster, Mark Mazzetti, and Edward T. Pound, "Truth and Consequences," *U.S. News & World Report*, June 9, 2003, http://www.usnews.com/usnews/news/articles/030609/9intell.htm.

15. Charles J. Hanley, "Point by Point, a Look Back at a 'Thick' File, a Fateful Six Months Later," Associated Press, August 7, 2003.

16. House Judiciary Committee Democratic Staff, "Exhibit B: Analysis of Powell Statements to U.N.," from *The Constitution in Crisis; The Downing Street Minutes and Deception, Manipulation, Torture, Retribution, and Coverups in the Iraq War*, December 20, 2005, http://www.house.gov/judiciary_democrats/iraqrept.html.

17. NBC News and *Wall Street Journal*, Survey, no. 6051, January 13–17, 2005, http://online.wsj.com/public/resources/media/poll20050119.pdf.

18. *Meet the Press*, "Vice President Dick Cheney Discusses 9/11 Anniversary, Iraq, Nation's Economy and Politics 2002" (transcript), September 8, 2002.

19. Powell, "Powell Addresses the UN Security Council."

20. George W. Bush, "President Says Saddam Hussein Must Leave Iraq Within 48 Hours" (transcript of national address), March 17, 2003, http://www.whitehouse.gov/news/releases/2003/03/20030317-7.html.

21. *Meet the Press*, "Vice President Dick Cheney Discusses a Possible War With Iraq" (transcript), March 16, 2003.

22. John J. Lumpkin, "Ex-CIA Officers Questioning Iraq Data," Associated Press, March 14, 2003; and Ray McGovern, "U.S. Troops' Safety Not a Bush Priority in Rush to War," *Capital Times* (Madison, WI), October 17, 2002, p. 15A.

23. Scott Ritter, "Is Iraq a True Threat to the U.S.?" *Boston Globe*, July 20, 2002, http://www.commondreams.org/views02/0721-02.htm.

24. Richard Stone, "U.N. Inspectors Find Wisps of Smoke But No Smoking Gun," *Science* 299, no. 5615 (March 28, 2003): 1967.

25. Dan Stober, "Checking False U.S. Leads Wasted Time, Source Says," *San Jose Mercury News*, p. A14.

26. Andrew Woodcock, "Blix Disappointed as War Starts," Press Association, March 20, 2003.

27. *Secretary Rumsfeld Remarks on ABC "This Week with George Stephanopoulis"* (transcript), United States Department of Defense, March 30, 2003, http://www.defenselink.mil/transcripts/2003/t03302003 _t0330sdabcsteph.html.

28. David Bloom, on *Today Show* (transcript), March 28, 2003.

29. William Branigan, "Chemical Threats Distract U.S. Troops," *Washington Post*, March 29, 2003, p. A22.

30. Bernard Weinraub, "Army Reports Iraq Is Moving Toxic Arms to Its Troops," *New York Times*, March 28, 2003, p. B6.

31. According to the final report of the Iraq Survey Group, which looked for banned weapons following the fall of Baghdad, "The group found that there was indeed a 'red line' defense for Baghdad, but it was a simple multi-ring conventional defense that quickly broke down under Coalition assault, and not the coordinated, prepared plan depicted in prewar intelligence reporting. . . . In addition, ISG could not find evidence that the defense plan explicitly called for [chemical weapons] use if triggered." See Iraq Survey Group, "Iraqi Chemical Weapons Programs: Iraq Survey Group Findings," *Iraq Survey Group Final Report*, September 30, 2004, http://www.globalsecurity.org/wmd/world/ iraq/cw-isg.htm.

32. *Evening Times* (Glasgow), "'Chemical Site' Discovered by U.S. Troops," April 4, 2003, p. 4.

33. David Kay, interview by Chris Matthews, *Hardball with Chris Matthews* (transcript), April 4, 2003.

34. David Usborne, "The Iraq Conflict: Vials Hold Explosives, Not Chemical Weapons," *Independent* (London), April 5, 2003, p. 5.

35. Jeffrey A. Dvorkin, "NPR News in Iraq: Getting the Full Story?"

National Public Radio website, April 11, 2003, http://www.npr.org/yourturn/ombudsman/2003/030411.html.

36. Dana Lewis, "Operation Iraqi Freedom" MSNBC special (transcript), April 7, 2003.

37. Richard Wallace, "WMDs? No, It's Just Farm Pesticide," *Mirror* (UK), April 8, 2003, http://www.mirror.co.uk/news/allnews/page.cfm?objectid=12821361&method=full.

38. Ken Auletta, "Vox Fox," *New Yorker*, May 26, 2003, p. 58.

39. Ibid.

40. *USA Today*, "15 minutes of war, as seen on TV news," April 9, 2003, p. 3D.

41. Matt Kelley, "U.S. Troops Find Suspected Chemical Plant Near An Najaf, Officials Say," Associated Press, March 23, 2003.

42. Fox News, "'Huge' Suspected Chemical Weapons Plant Found in Iraq," March 24, 2003, http://www.foxnews.com/story/0,2933,81935,00.html.

43. Carl Prine, "Team Arrives at Nuclear Plant to Hunt for Plutonium," *Pittsburgh Tribune-Review*, April 10, 2003, http://www.pittsburghlive.com/x/tribune-review/middleeastreports/prine/s_128508.html.

44. Fox News, "Weapons-Grade Plutonium Possibly Found at Iraqi Nuke Complex," April 11, 2003, http://www.foxnews.com/story/0,2933,83821,00.html.

45. "The Big Story with John Gibson," Fox News (transcript), April 10, 2003.

46. *Hannity and Colmes* "U.N. Iraqi Ambassador Leaves New York" (transcript), Fox News, April 11, 2003.

47. Paul Vallely, interview by Bill O'Reilly, "The O'Reilly Factor" (transcript), Fox News, May 8, 2003.

48. Program on International Policy Attitudes/Knowledge Networks Poll, University of Maryland, "Strong Majority Continues to Approve of War with Iraq" (news release), May 30, 2003, http://www.pipa.org/OnlineReports/Iraq/IraqFindWMD_May03/IraqFindWMD_May03_pr.pdf.

49. Glenn Kessler and Dana Milbank, "Administration Now Turns to Finding Prohibited Weapons," *Washington Post*, April 10, 2003, p. A36.

50. Ari Fleischer, White House press briefing (transcript), April 10, 2003.

51. Ari Fleischer, White House press briefing (transcript), April 22, 2003, http://www.whitehouse.gov/news/releases/2003/04/20030422-5.html.

52. BBC, "Blix Criticizes Coalition Over Iraq Weapons," June 6, 2003, http://news.bbc.co.uk/1/hi/world/americas/2967598.stm.

53. Barton Gellman, "Frustrated, U.S. Arms Team to Leave Iraq," *Washington Post*, May 10, 2003, p. A1, http://www.washingtonpost.com/ac2/wp-dyn/A40212-2003May10.

54. Barton Gellman, "Odyssey of Frustration," *Washington Post*, May 18, 2003, p. A1, http://www.veteransforpeace.org/Odyssey_of_Frustration_051803.htm.

55. Mike Allen, "Bush: 'We Found' Banned Weapons," *Washington Post*, May 31, 2003, p. A1, http://www.washingtonpost.com/ac2/wp-dyn/A60140-2003May30.

56. Douglas Jehl, "Iraqi Trailers Said to Make Hydrogen, Not Biological Arms," *New York Times*, August 9, 2003, p. A1. See also Peter Beaumont, Antony Barnett, and Gaby Hinsliff, "Iraqi Mobile Labs Nothing to Do with Germ Warfare, Report Finds," *Guardian* (UK), June 15, 2003, http://observer.guardian.co.uk/international/story/0,6903,977853,00.html.

57. Barton Gellman, "Iraq's Arsenal Was Only on Paper," *Washington Post*, January 7, 2004, p. A1, http://www.washingtonpost.com/ac2/wp-dyn/A60340-2004Jan6.

58. *CNN Late Edition with Wolf Blitzer* (transcript), CNN, June 1, 2003.

59. Bill Gertz and Rowan Scarborough, "Inside the Ring," *Washington Times*, August 1, 2003, p. A5, http://www.washtimes.com/national/20030731-110148-4800r.htm.

60. George W. Bush, "President Bush Discusses Top Priorities for the U.S." (transcript of news conference), July 30, 2003, http://whitehouse.fed.us/news/releases/2003/07/20030730-1.html.

61. Condoleezza Rice, interview by Gwen Ifill, *Newshour with Jim Lehrer* (transcript), July 30, 2003, http://www.pbs.org/newshour/bb/white_house/july-dec03/rice_7-30.html.

62. "Senators Hold Media Availability Following Closed Armed Services Committee Hearing on the Iraq Survey Group" (transcript), FDCH Political Transcripts, Washington, D.C., July 31, 2003.

63. "David Kay Holds Media Availability Following Closed Senate Intelligence Committee Hearing" (transcript), FDCH Political Transcripts, Washington, D.C., July 31, 2003.

64. Bryan Burrough, Evgenia Peretz, David Rose, and David Wise, "The Path to War," *Vanity Fair*, May 2004, p. 228.

65. Bob Drogin, "U.S. Suspects It Received False Iraq Arms Tips," *Los Angeles Times*, August 28, 2003, p. A1, http://truthout.org/docs_03/082903E.shtml.

66. Ibid.

67. Colin L. Powell, interview by Tim Russert, *Meet the Press* (transcript), September 7, 2003, http://www.state.gov/secretary/former/powell/remarks/2003/23857.htm.

68. Walter Pincus and Dana Priest, "Iraq Weapons Report Won't Be Conclusive," *Washington Post*, September 25, 2003, p. A1.

69. *Fox on the Record with Greta Van Susteren,* "Analysis with Mansoor Ijaz" (transcript), September 18, 2003.

70. David Kay, "Statement by David Kay on the *Interim Progress Report on the Activities of the Iraq Survey Group* (ISG) before the House Permanent Select Committee on Intelligence, the House Committee on Appropriations, Subcommittee on Defense, and the Senate Select Committee on Intelligence," October 2, 2003, http://www.cia.gov/cia/public_affairs/speeches/2003/david_kay_10022003.html.

71. *NBC Nightly News,* "No Weapons of Mass Destruction Found in Iraq" (transcript), October 2, 2003.

72. George W. Bush, interview by Diane Sawyer, *Good Morning America* (transcript), December 17, 2003.

73. William Langiewiesche, "The Wrath of Khan," *Atlantic Monthly,* November 2005, http://www.theatlantic.com/doc/prem/200511/aq-khan.

74. Gellman, "Iraq's Arsenal Was Only on Paper."

75. General Hussein Kamel, meeting with Professor M. Zifferero (IAEA) and Nikita Smidovich (UNSCOM) in Amman, Jordan, August 22, 1995 (transcript), pp. 12–13, http://www.fair.org/press-releases/kamel.pdf. For a

discussion of Hussein Kamel's revelations, see Sheldon Rampton and John Stauber, *Weapons of Mass Deception* (New York: Tarcher/Penguin, 2003), pp. 81–84.

76. Gellman, "Iraq's Arsenal Was Only on Paper."

77. Burrough, et al., "The Path to War."

78. Armed Services Committee, United States Senate, Hearing on Iraqi Weapons of Mass Destruction and Related Programs (transcript), FDCH Political Transcripts, January 28, 2004.

79. Charles Duelfer, "Realizing Saddam's Veiled WMD Intent," from *Comprehensive Report of the Special Advisor to the DCI on Iraq's WMD*, September 30, 2004, p. 64, http://www.globalsecurity.org/wmd/library/report/2004/isg-final-report/isg-final-report_vol1_rsi-06.htm.

80. Lawrence H. Silberman and Charles S. Robb, "Chapter One: Iraq," from *Report to the President of the Commission on the Intelligence Capabilities of the United States Regarding Weapons of Mass Destruction*, March 31, 2005, p. 45, http://govinfo.library.unt.edu/wmd/report/wmd_report.pdf.

81. Ibid.

82. Members of the Commission on the Intelligence Capabilities of the United States Regarding Weapons of Mass Destruction, letter to President George W. Bush, March 31, 2005.

Chapter Four: **Our Man in Baghdad**

1. Jane Mayer, "The Manipulator," *New Yorker*, June 7, 2004, http://www.newyorker.com/fact/content/?040607fa_fact1.

2. Ibid.

3. Douglas Jehl, "Agency Belittles Information Given by Iraqi Defectors," *New York Times*, September 29, 2003, p. A1.

4. Mark Hosenball and Michael Hirsh, "Chalabi: A Questionable Use of U.S. Funding," *Newsweek*, April 5, 2004, p. 6.

5. Kevin Fedarko, "Saddam's CIA Coup," *Time*, September 23, 1996, p. 43.

6. Mark Atkinson, "Propagandist for Hire," and "The CIA's Secret War in Iraq," ABC News, February 7, 1998, http://more.abcnews.go.com/

sections/world/cia/rendon.html and http://more.abcnews.go.com/sections/
world/cia/plot.htm. In his interview with Jane Mayer in 2004, however,
Francis Brooke suggested that the real amount spent may have been substantially more than ABC reported. "We tried to burn through forty million dollars a year," he said. See Mayer, "The Manipulator."

7. Mayer, "The Manipulator."

8. Ibid.

9. "PR Week Awards 2003: Specialist & Technique—the Ellwood &
Ellwood Award—Public Affairs," *PR Week*, October 30, 2003, http://
www.prweek.com/us/search/article/194036/prweek-awards-2003-special-
ist-amp-technique-ellwood-amp-ellwood-award-public-affairs.

10. Robin Wright, "Hapless Hussein Opposition Has U.S. Looking Elsewhere," *Los Angeles Times*, March 20, 2001, p. A1, http://www.wadinet
.de/news/iraq/nw68_hapless.htm.

11. Office of Inspector General, United States Department of State and
the Broadcasting Board of Governors, *Review of Awards to Iraqi National
Congress Support Foundation*, report number 01-FMA-R-092, September
2001, http://oig.state.gov/documents/organization/7508.pdf. See also
Karen DeYoung and Walter Pincus, "Rhetoric Fails to Budge Policy
on Iraq," *Washington Post*, January 24, 2002, p. A1, http://www
.washingtonpost.com/ac2/wp-dyn/A28324-2002Jan23.

12. General Accounting Office, *Issues Affecting Funding of Iraqi National Congress Support Foundation*, report GAO-04-559, April 2004,
p. 1, http://www.gao.gov/new.items/d04559.pdf.

13. Mayer, "The Manipulator."

14. Jonathan S. Landay and Tish Wells, "Iraqi Exile Group Fed False Information to News Media," Knight-Ridder, March 16, 2004, http://www
.veteransforpeace.org/Iraq_exile_group_031604.htm. See also Mark Hosenball and Michael Isikoff, "Exclusive: Cheney and the 'Raw' Intelligence," *Newsweek*, December 15, 2003, p. 8.

15. Chris Hedges, "Defectors Cite Iraqi Training for Terrorism," *New
York Times*, November 8, 2001. Hedges's story did not identify al-Qurairy
by name, but this information appeared in subsequent news stories that
used him as a source.

16. David Rose, "Inside Saddam's Terror Regime," *Vanity Fair*, January
21, 2002.

17. David Rose, "An Inconvenient Iraqi," *Vanity Fair*, January 2003, p. 70.

18. Douglas McCollam, "The List: How Chalabi Played the Press," *Columbia Journalism Review*, July/August 2004, http://www.cjr.org/issues/2004/4/mccollam-list.asp.

19. Bryan Burrough, Evgenia Peretz, David Rose, and David Wise, "The Path to War," *Vanity Fair*, May 2004, p. 228.

20. *Frontline*, "Gunning for Saddam: Interviews: An Iraqi Lt. General," http://www.pbs.org/wgbh/pages/frontline/shows/gunning/interviews/general.html.

21. Jack Fairweather, "Heroes in Error," *Mother Jones*, March/April 2006, http://www.motherjones.com/news/feature/2006/03/heroes_in_error.html.

22. Seymour M. Hersh, "Selective Intelligence," *New Yorker*, May 12, 2003, http://www.newyorker.com/printables/fact/030512fa_fact.

23. Select Committee on Intelligence, United States Senate, *Report of the Select Committee on Intelligence on the U.S. Intelligence Community's Prewar Intelligence Assessments on Iraq*, July 9, 2004, p. 332, http://www.gpoaccess.gov/serialset/creports/iraq.html.

24. Stephen F. Hayes, "Saddam's Terror Training Camps," *Weekly Standard*, January 16, 2006.

25. Select Committee, *Report of the Select Committee on Intelligence*, p. 95.

26. Ibid, p. 105.

27. Ibid, pp. 193–94.

28. Ibid, p. 479.

29. Bob Drogin and Greg Miller, "'Curveball' Debacle Reignites CIA Feud," *Los Angeles Times*, April 2, 2005, http://www.commondreams.org/headlines05/0402-01.htm.

30. Select Committee, *Report of the Select Committee on Intelligence*, pp. 194–95, http://www.gpoaccess.gov/serialset/creports/pdf/s108-301/sec12.pdf. For a critique of the Silberman-Robb report, see David Isenberg, "See, Hear and Speak No Incompetence: An Analysis of the Findings of the Commission on the Intelligence Capabilities of the United States Regarding Weapons of Mass Destruction," British American Security Information Council, October 2005, http://www.basicint.org/pubs/Research/05WMD.pdf.

31. Bob Drogin and Greg Miller, "Iraqi Defector's Tales Bolstered U.S. Case for War," *Los Angeles Times*, March 28, 2004, p. A1. See also Douglas Jehl, "Doubts on Informant Deleted in Senate Text," *New York Times*, July 13, 2004, http://www.nytimes.com/2004/07/13/politics/13reda.html.

32. Lawrence H. Silberman and Charles S. Robb, *Report to the President of the Commission on the Intelligence Capabilities of the United States Regarding Weapons of Mass Destruction*, March 31, 2005, p. 108, http://govinfo.library.unt.edu/wmd/report/wmd_report.pdf.

33. Ibid, p. 108.

34. Judith Miller, "Iraqi Tells of Renovations at Sites for Chemical and Nuclear Arms," *New York Times*, December 20, 2001, p. A1.

35. Jonathan S. Landay, "Iraqi Source for Weapons Claims Shaky," Knight Ridder, May 18, 2004.

36. Judith Miller and Michael R. Gordon, "U.S. Says Hussein Intensifies Quest for A-Bomb Parts," *New York Times*, September 8, 2002, p. A1.

37. Judith Miller and Michael R. Gordon, "White House Lists Iraq Steps to Build Banned Weapons," *New York Times*, September 13, 2002, p. A13.

38. Judith Miller, "Verification Is Difficult at Best, Say the Experts, and Maybe Impossible," *New York Times*, September 18, 2002, p. A18.

39. Hersh, "Selective Intelligence."

40. Judith Miller, "U.S. Faulted Over Its Efforts to Unite Iraqi Dissidents," *New York Times*, October 2, 2002, p. A16.

41. Judith Miller, "Defectors Bolster U.S. Case Against Iraq, Officials Say," *New York Times*, January 24, 2003, p. A11.

42. Howard Kurtz, "Embedded Reporter's Role in Army Unit's Actions Questioned by Military," *Washington Post*, June 25, 2003, p. C1, http://www.washingtonpost.com/ac2/wp-dyn/A28385-2003Jun24. Kurtz was not the only journalist to quote complaints about Miller from soldiers with whom she was embedded. See also William E. Jackson, Jr., "Miller's Latest Tale Questioned—When Will 'NY Times' Get Her off WMD Trail?" *Editor & Publisher Online*, September 23, 2003, http://www.commondreams.org/views03/0923-14.htm.

43. Howard Kurtz, "Intra-Times Battle over Iraqi Weapons," *Washington Post*, May 26, 2003, p. C1.

44. Judith Miller, "Illicit Arms Kept Till Eve of War, an Iraqi Scientist Is Said to Assert," *New York Times*, April 21, 2003, p. A1, http://www.nytimes.com/2003/04/21/international/worldspecial/21CHEM.html.

45. Sridhar Pappu, "Off the Record," *New York Observer*, April 28, 2003, p. 6.

46. Judith Miller, "A Chronicle of Confusion in the U.S. Hunt for Hussein's Chemical and Germ Weapons," *New York Times*, July 20, 2003, p. A12.

47. "From the Editors: The Times and Iraq," *New York Times*, May 26, 2004, p. A10, http://www.nytimes.com/2004/05/26/international/middleeast/26FTE_NOTE.html.

48. Judith Miller, "Remnants of Chemical Site Found," *New York Times*, April 24, 2003, p. A4.

49. Jack Schafer, "The *Times* Scoops That Melted," *Slate*, July 25, 2003, http://www.slate.com/id/2086110.

50. Daniel Okrent, "The Times and Judith Miller's WMD Coverage"(Weblog posting), *New York Times* forums, entry #21, March 25, 2004, http://forums.nytimes.com/top/opinion/readersopinions/forums/thepubliceditor/danielokrent/index.html?offset=27&page=previous.

51. "The Times and Iraq."

52. Daniel Okrent, "Weapons of Mass Destruction? Or Mass Distraction?" *New York Times*, May 30, 2004, http://www.nytimes.com/2004/05/30/weekinreview/30bott.html.

53. Bill Keller, e-mail to staff of the *New York Times*, Associated Press, October 21, 2005, http://www.msnbc.msn.com/id/9778787/.

54. Jim Romanesko, "There's a Scandal Hidden in Miller's Report," Poynter Forums, October 16, 2005, http://poynter.org/forum/view_post.asp?id=10495.

55. Judith Miller, "My Four Hours Testifying in the Federal Grand Jury Room," *New York Times*, October 16, 2005, p. 31.

56. Romanesko, "Scandal Hidden in Miller's Report."

57. Jack Fairweather, "Chalabi Stands by Faulty Intelligence that Toppled Saddam's Regime," *Telegraph* (UK), February 19, 2004.

58. Bob Drogin, "Suspicion of Chalabi Deception Intensifies," *Los Angeles Times*, May 23, 2004, p. A1.

59. "Oil from Iraq: An Israeli Pipedream?" *Jane's Middle East/Africa News*, April 16, 2003, http://www.janes.com/regional_news/africa_middle _east/news/fr/fr030416_1_n.shtml.

60. John Dizard, "How Chalabi Conned the Neocons," *Salon.com*, May 4, 2004, http://www.salon.com/news/feature/2004/05/04/chalabi/index .html.

61. Mark Hosenball, "Intelligence: A Double Game," *Newsweek*, May 10, 2004, http://msnbc.msn.com/id/4881157/.

62. Walter Pincus and Dana Priest, "On Hill, Rice Pledges Probe of Alleged Chalabi Leak," *Washington Post*, June 3, 2004, p. A1, http://www .washingtonpost.com/wp-dyn/articles/A11043-2004Jun2.html.

63. Jonathan Finer and Robin Wright, "Chalabi Ready for U.S. Visit, Another Shot at Limelight," *Washington Post*, November 5, 2005, http:// www.washingtonpost.com/wp-dyn/content/article/2005/11/06/ AR2005110600321.html.

Chapter Five: **Rewriting History**

1. George W. Bush, "President Commemorates Veterans Day, Discusses War on Terror" (transcript of speech given at Tobyhanna Army Depot, Tobyhanna, PA), November 11, 2005, http://www.whitehouse.gov/ news/releases/2005/11/20051111-1.html.

2. George W. Bush and Kofi Annan, "President Reaffirms Strong Position on Liberia" (transcript of remarks made in photo opportunity at the Oval Office), July 14, 2003, http://www.whitehouse.gov/news/releases/ 2003/07/20030714-3.html.

3. Dana Priest and Dana Milbank, "President Defends Allegation on Iraq," *Washington Post*, July 15, 2003, p. A1, http://www.washingtonpost .com/ac2/wp-dyn?pagename=article&contentId=A56336-2003Jul14.

4. Bob Graham, "What I Knew Before the Invasion," *Washington Post*, November 20, 2005, p. B7, http://www.washingtonpost.com/wp-dyn/ content/article/2005/11/18/AR2005111802397.html.

5. Henry Waxman, *Iraq on the Record* (online database), http://demo-crats.reform.house.gov/IraqOnTheRecord. For a longer excerpt from the

2002 National Intelligence Estimate, see United States Department of Defense, "Defense Agency Issues Excerpt on Iraqi Chemical Warfare Program" (news release), June 9, 2003, http://www.fas.org/irp/news/2003/06/dod060703.html.

6. Bloomberg News, "Pentagon in 2002 Found 'No Reliable' Iraq Arms Data," June 6, 2003, http://www.truthout.org/docs_03/060703B.shtml.

7. Michael White, "Putin Demands Proof Over Iraqi Weapons," *Guardian* (UK), October 12, 2002, http://www.guardian.co.uk/international/story/0,3604,810627,00.html.

8. BBC, "Paris Pact Urges Inspection Boost," February 11, 2003, http://news.bbc.co.uk/1/hi/world/europe/2746459.stm.

9. CNN *Newsnight with Aaron Brown*, "Will France, Germany, Russia Thwart Possible U.S. Plans for War?" (transcript), February 10, 2003, http://transcripts.cnn.com/TRANSCRIPTS/0302/10/asb.00.html.

10. Philip Smucker, "Once High, Arab Hopes for President Bush Fall," *Christian Science Monitor*, February 19, 2003, http://csmweb2.emcweb.com/2003/0219/p01s04-wome.html.

11. Brent Scowcroft, "Don't Attack Saddam," *Wall Street Journal*, August 15, 2002, p. A12, http://www.wagingpeace.org/articles/2002/08/15_scowcroft_dont-attack.htm.

12. Fox News, "Transcript: Lawrence Eagleburger on FNS," August 19, 2002, http://www.foxnews.com/story/0,2933,60704,00.html.

13. Todd S. Purdum and Patrick E. Tyler, "Top Republicans Break with Bush on Iraq Strategy," *New York Times*, August 15, 2005, p. 1, http://www.truthout.org/docs_02/08.17A.gop.no.irq.htm.

14. Warren P. Strobel, Jonathan S. Landay, and John Wolcott, "Some in Bush Administration Have Misgivings About Iraq Policy," October 8, 2002, Knight Ridder, http://www.realcities.com/mld/krwashington/news/special_packages/iraq/intelligence/11922658.htm.

15. Bob Woodward, *Plan of Attack* (New York: Simon & Schuster, 2004), pp. 281, 292. See also Tommy Franks, *American Soldier* (New York: HarperCollins, 2004), p. 563.

16. Robert Dreyfuss, "The Pentagon Muzzles the CIA," *American Prospect* 13, no. 22 (December 16, 2002), http://www.prospect.org/print-friendly/print/V13/22/dreyfuss-r.html. See also Robert Dreyfuss and

Jason Vest, "The Lie Factory," *Mother Jones*, January/February 2004, http://www.motherjones.com/news/feature/2004/01/12_405.html.

17. Eric Schmitt and Thom Shanker, "Pentagon Sets Up Intelligence Unit," *New York Times*, October 24, 2002, p. A1.

18. Nicholas D. Kristof, "Save Our Spooks," *New York Times*, May 30, 2003, p. A27.

19. Laura Blumenfeld, "Former Aide Takes Aim at War on Terror," *Washington Post*, June 16, 2003, p. A1, http://www.washingtonpost.com/ac2/wp-dyn/A62941-2003Jun15.

20. Paul R. Pillar, "Intelligence, Policy, and the War in Iraq," *Foreign Affairs*, March/April 2006, http://www.foreignaffairs.org/20060301faessay85202/paul-r-pillar/intelligence-policy-and-the-war-in-iraq.html.

21. House of Commons, *Review of Intelligence on Weapons of Mass Destruction*, July 14, 2004, p. 164, 167–69, http://www.archive2.official -documents.co.uk/document/deps/hc/hc898/898.pdf.

22. *Times* (UK), "The Secret Downing Street Memo," May 1, 2005, http://www.timesonline.co.uk/article/0,,19809-1593637,00.html. See also the Downing Street Memo website, http://www.downingstreetmemo .com. Some U.S. commentators have argued that the phrase "fixed around the policy" has a different meaning in the British dialect of English than American readers would expect. However, this interpretation is strongly rejected by Michael Smith, the British reporter who originally published the memo: "This is a real joke. I do not know anyone in the UK who took it to mean anything other than fixed as in fixed a race, fixed an election, fixed the intelligence. If you fix something, you make it the way you want it." See "The Downing Street Memo" (online discussion transcript), *Washington Post* online, June 16, 2005, http://www.washingtonpost.com/wp-dyn/content/discussion/2005/06/14/ DI2005061401261.html.

23. Sheldon Rampton and John Stauber, *Weapons of Mass Deception: The Uses of Propaganda in Bush's War on Iraq* (New York: Tarcher/Penguin, 2003), pp. 96–98.

24. Glenn Frankel, "Blair Acknowledges Flaws in Iraq Dossier," *Washington Post*, February 8, 2003, http://www.washingtonpost.com/ac2/wp -dyn/A42276-2003Feb7.

25. BBC, "Leaked Report Rejects Iraqi Al-Qaeda Link," February 5, 2003, http://news.bbc.co.uk/2/hi/uknews/2727471.stm. See also Raymond Whitaker, "MI6 and the CIA: The Enemy Within," *New Zealand Herald*, February 9, 2003, http://www.nzherald.co.nz/storydisplay.cfm?storyID=3100174.

26. BBC, "Cook's Resignation Speech," March 18, 2003, http://news.bbc.co.uk/1/hi/uk_politics/2859431.stm.

27. Steve Rendall and Tara Broughel, "Amplifying Officials, Squelching Dissent," FAIR (Fairness and Accuracy in Reporting) *Extra!*, May/June 2003, http://www.fair.org/index.php?page=1145.

28. Fox News, "Transcript: Janeane Garofalo on *Fox News Sunday*," February 24, 2003, http://www.foxnews.com/story/0,2933,79351,00.html.

29. Joshua Micah Marshall, "Talking Points Memo" (weblog posting), July 28, 2003, http://www.talkingpointsmemo.com/archives/001026.php.

30. Anthony Shadid, "At Least 6 Policemen Killed in Iraq Battle," *Washington Post*, February 11, 2005, p. A18.

31. Jean-Marc Mojon, "Salman Pak, Iraq's New Lawless Hotspot," Agence France-Presse, February 11, 2005, http://www.middle-east-online.com/english/?id=12667.

32. Sabrina Tavirnise, "As Iraqi Shiites Police Sunnis, Rough Justice Feeds Bitterness," *New York Times*, February 6, 2006, p. A4.

33. Reuters, "Mubarak Warns of '100 Bin Ladens,'" March 31, 2003, http://www.cnn.com/2003/WORLD/meast/03/31/iraq.egypt.mubarak.reut.

34. Coleen Rowley, open letter to FBI director Robert S. Mueller III, February 26, 2003, http://www.commondreams.org/headlines03/0306-07.htm.

35. Ramesh Ponnuru, "Whistle Stop," *National Review*, March 7, 2003, http://www.nationalreview.com/ponnuru/ponnuru030703.asp.

36. Richard Armitage and J. Cofer Black, news conference on the release of the State Department's annual *Patterns of Global Terrorism* report (transcript), Federal News Services April 29, 2004.

37. Peter Slevin, "New 2003 Data: 625 Terrorism Deaths, Not 307," *Washington Post*, June 23, 2004, p. A1. Some people have speculated that the original undercount was deliberate, but former CIA analyst Larry Johnson (a critic of the Bush administration) thinks the errors are so glaring that they suggest incompetence rather than intentional concealment.

For his comments, see Corine Hegland, "Terrorism Body Counts," *National Journal* 36, no. 25 (June 19, 2004).

38. Krishnadev Calamur, "New Terror Report Shows Spike in Attacks," United Press International, June 22, 2004.

39. CNN, "Terror Threat to U.S. Called 'Significant,'" April 27, 2005, http://www.cnn.com/2005/US/04/27/terror.report. See also Philip Zelikow and John Brennan, "Remarks on Release of *Country Reports on Terrorism* for 2004" (transcript), U.S. Department of State, April 27, 2005, http://www.state.gov/s/ct/rls/rm/45279.htm.

40. Richard Boucher, United States State Department press briefing (transcript), April 18, 2005, http://usinfo.state.gov/xarchives/display.html?p =washfile-english&y=2005&m=April&x=20050418174523xjsnommis0 .4271356&t=is/is-latest.html.

41. Katherine Schrader, "Terror Attacks Near 3,200 in 2004 Count," Associated Press, July 6, 2005, http://www.sfgate.com/cgi-bin/article.cgi?file −/n/a/2005/07/05/national/w162402D28.DTL.

42. Michael Scheuer, *Imperial Hubris: Why the West Is Losing the War on Terror* (Dulles, VA: Brassey's, 2004), pp. 213–14.

43. United States Department of Defense, press briefing (transcript), June 30, 2005, http://www.defenselink.mil/transcripts/2005/tr20050630 -3221.html.

44. Warren P. Strobel, "Iraq Seen Emerging as Prime Training Ground for Terrorists," Knight Ridder, July 4, 2005, http://www.realcities.com/ mld/krwashington/12052900.htm.

45. Douglas Jehl, "Iraq May Be Prime Place for Training of Militants, CIA Report Concludes," *New York Times*, June 22, 2005, p. A10.

46. Kenneth Adelman, "Cakewalk in Iraq," *Washington Post*, February 13, 2002, p. A27, http://www.washingtonpost.com/ac2/wp-dyn/A1996 -2002Feb12.

47. "Saddam's Ultimate Solution," *Wide Angle* (transcript), July 11, 2002, http://www.pbs.org/wnet/wideangle/shows/saddam/transcript3.html.

48. *Meet the Press*, "Vice President Dick Cheney Discusses a Possible War with Iraq" (transcript), March 16, 2003.

49. *Today*, "Lieutenant General William Odom, Former Director, National Security Agency, Discusses the Iraq War" (transcript), April 29, 2004.

Chapter Six: **Not Counting the Dead**

1. Patrick J. Sloyan, "War Without Death," *San Francisco Chronicle*, November 17, 2002, http://www.sfgate.com/cgi-bin/article.cgi?file=/chronicle/archive/2002/11/17/IN178228.DTL.

2. Patrick J. Sloyan, "Buried Alive; U.S. Tanks Used Plows to Kill Thousands in Gulf War Trenches," *Newsday*, September 12, 1991, p. 1.

3. Sloyan, "War Without Death."

4. Peter Turnley, "The Unseen Gulf War," *The Digital Journalist*, December 2002, http://www.digitaljournalist.org/issue0212/pt_intro.html.

5. Carl Conetta, *The Wages of War: Iraqi Combatant and Noncombatant Fatalities in the 2003 Conflict*, Project on Defense Alternatives Research Monograph Number 8, October 20, 2003, http://www.comw.org/pda/0310rm8ap2.html.

6. Michael Oreskes, "Selling of a Military Strike: Coffins Arriving as Bush Speaks," *New York Times*, December 22, 1989, p. A18.

7. Ron Martz, "Embed Catches Heat," *Editor & Publisher*, May 15, 2003, http://www.editorandpublisher.com/eandp/news/article_display.jsp?vnu_content_id=1886508.

8. Ibid.

9. Iraq Coalition Casualty Count, http://icasualties.org/oif.

10. George W. Bush, "President Announces Combat Operations in Iraq Have Ended" (transcript of speech by President George W. Bush aboard the USS *Abraham Lincoln*), May 1, 2003, http://www.state.gov/p/nea/rls/rm/20203.htm.

11. Dana Milbank, "Curtains Ordered for Media Coverage of Returning Coffins," *Washington Post*, October 21, 2003, p. A3, http://www.informationclearinghouse.info/article6078.htm.

12. Ibid.

13. Greg Mitchell, "Media Underplays U.S. Death Toll in Iraq," *Editor and Publisher*, July 17, 2003.

14. James Ridgeway, "The Mourning Show," *Village Voice*, November 5–11, 2003, http://www.villagevoice.com/news/0345,mondo2,48394,6.html.

15. Denise Grady, "Struggling Back from War's Once-Deadly Wounds,"

New York Times, January 22, 2006, http://www.nytimes.com/2006/01/22/national/22wounded.html.

16. Vernon Lobe, "Number of Wounded in Action on Rise," *Washington Post*, September 2, 2003, p. A1, http://www.sfgate.com/cgi-bin/article.cgi?file=/chronicle/archive/2003/09/03/MN280141.DTL.

17. Disabled American Veterans, Department of Ohio, Information bulletin, March 2004, http://www.ohiodav.org/March,%202004.htm.

18. Gene Collier, "Wounded U.S. Veterans Get a Raw Deal at Home," *Pittsburgh Post-Gazette*, February 8, 2004, p. G12.

19. David W. Gorman, letter to Defense Secretary Donald Rumsfeld, January 2, 2004, http://releases.usnewswire.com/GetRelease.asp?id=24824.

20. CNN, "Forces: U.S. & Coalition/Casualties," http://www.cnn.com/SPECIALS/2003/iraq/forces/casualties/ and *Washington Post*, "Faces of the Fallen: U.S. Fatalities in Iraq," http://www.washingtonpost.com/wp-srv/world/iraq/casualties/facesofthefallen.htm.

21. The *Army Times* is continuing to update its memorial to fallen soldiers on the Web, at http://www.militarycity.com/valor/.

22. Hal Bernton, "The Somber Task of Honoring the Fallen," *Seattle Times*, April 18, 2004, http://seattletimes.nwsource.com/html/nationworld/2001906489_kuwait18m.html.

23. Tami Silicio, "Mission Statement—How I Feel About the Picture Itself and What It Means," http://www.tamisilicio.net.

24. Charles Geraci, "*Seattle Times* Reports Favorable Response to 'Coffins' Photo," *Editor and Publisher*, April 19, 2004.

25. Greg Mitchell, "Father Who Believes Son Is in 'Coffin' Photo Thanks 'Seattle Times' for Running It," *Editor and Publisher*, April 28, 2004.

26. Greg Mitchell, "When Will the First Newspaper Call for a Pullout in Iraq?" *Editor and Publisher*, May 7, 2004.

27. Al Neuharth, "Should Cowboy Bush Ride into the Sunset?" *USA Today*, May 13, 2004, http://www.usatoday.com/news/opinion/columnist/neuharth/2004-05-13-neuharth_x.htm.

28. Greg Mitchell, "Cindy Sheehan, Bill Mitchell and the Lost Boys," *Editor and Publisher*, August 11, 2005.

29. Steve Yelvington, "Tami Silicio and thememoryhole.org" (weblog posting), April 24, 2004, http://www.yelvington.com/item.php?id=428.

30. National Security Archive, "Return of the Fallen," Electronic Briefing Book No. 152, http://www.gwu.edu/nsarchiv/NSAEBB/NSAEBB152.

31. Sinclair Broadcast Group, statement to the press, April 29, 2004, http://www.newscentral.tv/station/statement.shtml.

32. Oliver Wendell Holmes, Sr., "Doings of the Sunbeam," *Atlantic Monthly* 12 (July 1863), pp. 11–12.

33. Warren P. Strobel, *Late-Breaking Foreign Policy: The News Media's Influence on Peace Operations* (Washington, D.C.: United States Institute of Peace Press, 1997), p. 26.

34. Josh White and Ann Scott Tyson, "Military Has Lost 2,000 In Iraq," *Washington Post*, October 26, 2005, p. A1, http://www.washingtonpost.com/wp-dyn/content/article/2005/10/25/AR2005102501185_pf.html.

35. Dexter Filkins and James Dao, "Afghan Battle Declared Over and Successful," *New York Times*, March 19, 2003, p. A1.

36. Agence France-Presse, "Bremer Takes on Critics of U.S.-Led Occupation of Iraq," August 12, 2003.

37. Guy Shields, "Coalition Provisional Authority Briefing to Include Background Briefing on Iraqi Compensation" (transcript of U.S. Defense Department press briefing), August 4, 2003. Federal News Service.

38. Ray Glenn, memo to the copy desk at the Panama City (Florida) *News Herald*, October 31, 2001; cited in Jim Romanesko's Media News, http://www.poynter.org/medianews/memos.htm; copy available in the Internet Archive for December 2, 2001, http://www.archive.org.

39. Human Rights Watch, "Off Target: The Conduct of the War and Civilian Casualties in Iraq," December 2003, http://www.hrw.org/reports/2003/usa1203/3.htm. See also Paul Wiseman, "Cluster Bombs Kill in Iraq After Shooting Ends," *USA Today*, December 16, 2003, http://www.usatoday.com/news/world/iraq/2003-12-10-cluster-bomb-cover_x.htm.

40. Sheldon Rampton and John Stauber, *Weapons of Mass Deception: The Uses of Propaganda in Bush's War on Iraq* (New York: Tarcher/Penguin, 2003), pp. 193–98.

41. Marc W. Herold, "A Dossier on Civilian Victims of United States' Aerial Bombing of Afghanistan," March 2002, http://www.cursor.org/stories/civilian_deaths.htm. For a discussion by Herold of his methodology and a comparison with some other efforts to tally civilian deaths in Afghanistan, see Marc Herold, "Counting the Dead," *Guardian* (UK),

August 8, 2002, http://www.guardian.co.uk/afghanistan/comment/story/0
,11447,770999,00.html.
42. Glenn Reynolds, "InstaPundit," weblog posting, March 22, 2003,
http://instapundit.com/archives/008364.php.
43. H. D. Miller, "Iraq Body Count," weblog posting, March 16, 2003,
http://travellingshoes.blogspot.com/2003_03_16_travellingshoes_archive
.html; David Adesnik, weblog posting, http://oxblog.blogspot.com/
2003_03_02_oxblog_archive.html; "Little Green Footballs," weblog
posting, November 16, 2002, http://www.littlegreenfootballs.com/
weblog/?entry=4732; Bruce Rolston, "Marc Herold: The Eternal Liar,"
Flit weblog, August 9, 2002, http://www.snappingturtle.net/flit/archives/
2002_08_09.html#000533. The most serious attempt to critique
Herold's results on methodological grounds rather than by pure
invective came from Joshua Muravchik, "The Professor Who Can't
Count Straight," *Weekly Standard*, August 26, 2002, http://www
.weeklystandard.com/Content/Public/Articles/000/000/001/565otmps.asp.
One of the most consistent accusations made by Herold's critics is that
some of his figures came from Taliban-controlled media or other non-
Western sources that they suspect of dishonestly inflating casualty figures. However, bias in the opposite direction might also be a factor in
the figures appearing in Western news reports, and in at least some of
the incidents in his database, figures supplied by the Taliban were actually *lower* than figures supplied by other observers. See Herold, "Counting the Dead."
44. For the details of Iraq Body Count's methodology, see http://www
.iraqbodycount.net/background.htm.
45. Iraq Body Count, "Dossier of Civilian Casualties in Iraq, 2003–2005"
(press release), July 2005, http://www.iraqbodycount.net/press/pr12.php.
46. Andres Oppenheimer, "Information Gap Helps Fuel Anti-
Americanism," *Miami Herald*, July 21, 2005, p. A10, http://www.miami
.com/mld/miamiherald/news/columnists/andres_oppenheimer/12183298
.htm.
47. Stephen Spruiell, "Bad Counts," *National Review*, July 26, 2005,
http://www.nationalreview.com/comment/spruiell200507260924.asp.
48. Following her death, Ruzicka's work is being continued by her organization, the Campaign for Innocent Victims in Conflict (CIVIC),

http://www.civicworldwide.org. The results of her research into civilian casualties are at http://civilians.info/iraq.

49. Christopher Albritton, "Our Heart and Conscience," Back to Iraq weblog, April 19, 2005, http://www.back-to-iraq.com/archives/2005/04/.

50. Debbie Schlussel, "Meet the Real Marla Ruzicka," *FrontPage Magazine*, April 25, 2005, http://www.frontpagemag.com/Articles/ReadArticle .asp?ID=17823.

51. Les Roberts, Riyadh Lafta, Richard Garfield, Jamal Khudhairi, and Gilbert Burnham, "Mortality Before and After the 2003 Invasion of Iraq: Cluster Sample Survey," *Lancet* 364, no. 9448 (November 20, 2004): 1857–64, http://www.indybay.org/uploads/lancet_10-29-04_article _on_iraq_casualties.pdf.

52. Marvin Olasky, "War or No War, Innocent People Will Die," Townhall, October 22, 2002, http://www.townhall.com/opinion/columns/ marvinolasky/2002/10/22/164696.html.

53. *This American Life*, "What's in a Number?" October 28, 2005, http:// www.thisamericanlife.org/pages/descriptions/05/300.html; audio stream available at http://www.thisamericanlife.org/ra/300.ram.

54. *Democracy Now!*, "Study Shows Civilian Death Toll in Iraq More Than 100,000" (transcript of interview with Les Roberts), December 14, 2005, http://www.democracynow.org/article.pl?sid=05/12/14/154251.

55. Lila Guterman, "Researchers Who Rushed into Print a Study of Iraqi Civilian Deaths Now Wonder Why It Was Ignored," *Chronicle of Higher Education*, January 27, 2005, http://chronicle.com/free/2005/01/ 2005012701n.htm.

56. Roberts, et al. "Mortality Before and After the 2003 Invasion of Iraq."

57. Richard Horton, "The War in Iraq: Civilian Casualties, Political Responsibilities," *Lancet* 364, no. 9448 (November 20, 2004): 1831, http:// www.indybay.org/uploads/lancet_10-29-04_article_on_iraq_casualties.pdf.

58. *This American Life*, "What's in a Number?"

59. Guterman, "Study of Iraqi Civilian Deaths."

60. Elizabeth Rosenthal, "Study Puts Iraqi Deaths of Civilians at 100,000," *New York Times*, October 29, 2004, p. A8.

61. Rob Stein, "100,000 Civilian Deaths Estimated in Iraq," *Washington Post*, October 29, 2004, p. A16.

62. Guterman, "Study of Iraqi Civilian Deaths."

63. *This American Life*, "What's in a Number?"

64. Edward Ericson, Jr., "A Controversial Report from Johns Hopkins Researchers Estimates Iraq Civilian Death Toll," *Baltimore City Paper*, November 17, 2004, http://www.citypaper.com/news/story.asp?id=9349.

65. Michael Fumento, "*Lancet* Civilian Death Report Kills the Truth," Tech Central Station, November 1, 2004, http://www.techcentralstation .com/110104H.html.

66. Tim Worstall, "The *Lancet*: A Casualty of Politics," Tech Central Station, October 29, 2004, http://www.techcentralstation.com/102904J .html; "The *Lancet*: A Casualty of Politics," Little Green Footballs weblog posting, October 29, 2004, http://www.littlegreenfootballs.com/ weblog/?entry=13334&only=yes; Shannon Love and Charles Johnson, "Bogus *Lancet* Study," weblog posting, October 29, 2004, http://www .chicagoboyz.net/archives/002543.html. For additional examples of the pro-war response, and responses to their attempts at methodological critiques, see the weblog of computer science professor Tim Lambert, at http://timlambert.org/category/lancetiraq.

67. CNN, "Bush: Iraqi Democracy Making Progress," December 12, 2005, http://www.cnn.com/2005/POLITICS/12/12/bush.iraq/.

Chapter Seven: **The Mirage of Victory**

1. Liat Radcliffe, "Ahmad Al-Rikaby" (interview), *Newsweek*, August 18, 2003, p. 58.

2. Bassem Mroue, "Internet Use Spreading Throughout Iraq," Associated Press, November 14, 2005, http://www.usatoday.com/tech/news/ 2005-11-14-iraq-internet_x.htm?csp=34.

3. Salam Pax's prewar weblog was called Where is Raed? http://dear _raed.blogspot.com. More recently, he has been blogging at Shut Up You Fat Whiner! http://justzipit.blogspot.com/.

4. Salam Pax, "A Post From Baghdad Station," blog post from Where is Raed? May 7, 2003, http://dear_raed.blogspot.com/2003_05_01_dear _raed_archive.html#200255082.

5. Ibid.

6. Salam Pax, Where is Raed? blog post, February 12, 2004, http://dear
_raed.blogspot.com/2004_02_01_dear_raed_archive.html#1076600574
07559034.

7. See http://raedinthemiddle.blogspot.com; http://afamilyinbaghdad
.blogspot.com; http://riverbendblog.blogspot.com; http://healing
iraq.blogspot.com; http://iraqataglance.blogspot.com; http://www
.messopotamian.blogspot.com; http://hammorabi.blogspot.com; http://
www.iraqthemodel.blogspot.com; http://baghdadgirl.blogspot.com.

8. See http://iraqblogcount.blogspot.com.

9. Omar Fadhil, "After the Election, Frustration Replaces Optimism,"
Iraq the Model weblog, January 5, 2006, http://iraqthemodel.blogspot
.com/2006/01/after-election-frustration-replaces.html.

10. Ali Fadhil, A Free Iraqi weblog, December 26, 2005, http://
afreeiraqi.blogspot.com/2005/12/i-wanted-to-say-something-about.html.
Note: Ali began blogging with his brothers at Iraq the Model, but beginning in December 2004 he has maintained A Free Iraqi as his own separate blog.

11. "Tight Rope," Messopotamian weblog, January 7, 2006, http://
messopotamian.blogspot.com/2006_01_01_messopotamian_archive.html
#113663402509210983.

12. "Iraq Is Far Away from Being FREE," Iraq at a Glance weblog,
December 22, 2005, http://iraqataglance.blogspot.com/2005_12_01
_iraqataglance_archive.html.

13. Paul Wolfowitz, interview by Sam Tannenhaus, *Vanity Fair* (transcript), May 9, 2003, posted on U.S. Department of Defense website, http://
www.defenselink.mil/transcripts/2003/tr20030509-depsecdef0223.html.

14. Allen G. Breed, "Soldier Who Turned Over Abuse Photos Says He
Agonized Before Reporting Abuse," Associated Press, August 6, 2004.

15. Major General Antonio Taguba, The "Taguba Report" on Treatment
of Abu Ghraib Prisoners In Iraq, Article 15-6 Investigation of the 800th
Military Police Brigade, 2005, http://news.findlaw.com/nytimes/docs/
iraq/tagubarpt.html.

16. Red Cross, *Report of the International Committee of the Red Cross
(ICRC) on the Treatment by Coalition Forces of Prisoners of War and
Other Protected Persons by the Geneva Conventions in Iraq During Arrest,*

Internment, and Interrogation, February 2004, http://msnbcmedia.msn
.com/i/msnbc/Sections/News/International%20News/Mideast%20and
%20N.%20Africa/Iraq%20conflict/Red%20Cross%20report.pdf.

17. Sharon Churcher, "Good Ol' Girl Who Enjoyed Cruelty," *Daily Telegraph* (Sydney, Australia), May 7, 2004, p. 4.

18. Hanna Rosin, "When Joseph Comes Marching Home," *Washington Post,* May 17, 2004, p. C1, http://www.washingtonpost.com/wp-dyn/articles/A32048-2004May16.html.

19. *Good Morning America,* "Specialist Joseph Darby: Family of Military Hero Interviewed" (transcript), August 16, 2004.

20. For an example, see "Moving and Patrols," Fun with Hand Grenades weblog, November 2, 2005, http://funwithhandgrenades.blogspot.com/2005/11/moving-and-patrols.html.

21. "Slang from Operation Iraqi Freedom," Global Security website, http://www.globalsecurity.org/military/ops/iraq-slang.htm.

22. CNN, "Former Aide: Powell WMD Speech 'Lowest Point in My Life,'" August 23, 2005, http://www.cnn.com/2005/WORLD/meast/08/19/powell.un.

23. Lawrence Wilkerson, "Weighing the Uniqueness of the Bush Administration's National Security Decision-Making Process: Boon or Danger to American Democracy?" New America Foundation, American Strategy Program Policy Forum (forum transcript), October 19, 2005, http://www.newamerica.net/Download_Docs/pdfs/Doc_File_2644_1.pdf.

24. "Italian PM Says He Tried to Dissuade Bush from Iraq War," *USA Today,* October 30, 2005, http://www.usatoday.com/news/world/2005-10-30-italy-iraq_x.htm.

25. William F. Buckley, Jr., "It Didn't Work," *National Review,* February 24, 2006, http://www.nationalreview.com/buckley/buckley200602241451.asp.

26. John P. Murtha, "The War in Iraq" (press release), November 17, 2005, http://www.house.gov/apps/list/press/pa12_murtha/pr051117iraq.html.

27. Thomas M. DeFrank, "Bushies Feeling the Boss' Wrath," New York *Daily News,* October 24, 2005, http://www.nydailynews.com/front/story/358714p-305660c.html.

28. Jeffrey P. Jones, "Three in Four Americans Think Civil War Likely in

Iraq," Gallup News Service, March 6, 2006, http://poll.gallup.com/content/default.aspx?ci=21778.

29. Daniel Yankelovich, "Poll Positions," *Foreign Affairs*, September/October 2005, p. 2, http://www.foreignaffairs.org/20050901faessay84501/daniel-yankelovich/poll-positions.html.

30. Andrew Kohut, "Bush's Concern Over Isolationism Reflects More Than Just Rhetoric," Pew Research Center for the People and the Press, February 3, 2006, http://pewresearch.org/obdeck/?ObDeckID=3.

31. *Fox News Sunday Roundtable* (transcript), February 26, 2006.

32. *Fox on the Record with Greta Van Susteren* (transcript), May 7, 2003.

INDEX

Index

© Laura J. Berger

About the Authors

SHELDON RAMPTON AND JOHN STAUBER BOTH work for the Center for Media and Democracy, a nonprofit organization that they began in 1993 to monitor and expose deceptive public relations campaigns and other propaganda sponsored by corporations and governments. They have coauthored five other books: *Toxic Sludge Is Good for You! Lies, Damn Lies and the Public Relations Industry* (1995); *Mad Cow U.S.A.* (1997); *Trust Us. We're Experts! How Industry Manipulates Science and Gambles with Your Future* (2001); *Weapons of Mass Deception: The Uses of Propaganda in Bush's War on Iraq* (2003); and *Banana Republicans: How the Right Wing Is Turning America into a One-Party State* (2004).

John Stauber founded the Center for Media and Democracy and its newsmagazine, *PR Watch*, and serves as the Center's executive director. He is an investigative writer, public speaker, and democracy activist, whose leadership on controversial issues began in high school, when he organized to stop the U.S. war on Vietnam and to support the first Earth Day. Since then, he has launched or worked with many public interest groups, including the Peoples Bicentennial Commission, Wisconsin Coordinating Council on Nicaragua, Foundation on Economic Trends, and Action Coalition for Media Education.

Sheldon Rampton is a graduate of Princeton University, who has a diverse background as newspaper reporter, activist, and author. In college, he studied writing under Joyce Carol Oates, E. L. Doctorow, and John McPhee. In addition to books written with John Stauber, he is the coauthor with Liz Chilsen of the 1998 book *Friends in Deed: The Story of US-Nicaragua Sister Cities*. Prior to joining the Center for Media and Democracy, he worked for the Wisconsin Coordinating Council on Nicaragua (www.wccnica.org) on the NICA Fund, a project that channels loans from U.S. investors to support economic development efforts in low-income Central American communities.

For further information about the authors, including archived copies of *PR Watch*, visit www.prwatch.org, or contact:

Center for Media and Democracy
520 University Avenue, Suite #227
Madison, WI 53703
Phone (608) 260-9713